TRINITY PSALTER

PSALMS 1-150

WORDS–ONLY EDITION

Special Thanks

The publishers are deeply grateful for the tireless work and kind cooperation of the following:

Pastor Terry Johnson, compiler and editor, Independent Presbyterian Church
Mrs. Laura Lee Sims, typesetting/layout, Independent Presbyterian Church
Mrs. Lori Lattner, typesetting/layout, Independent Presbyterian Church
Mr. Charles McBurney, consultant, RPCNA
Rev. Thomas R. Patete, executive director, Great Commission Publications
Dr. Charles Dunahoo, director, Committee for Christian Education and
     Publications, PCA
Mr. John Dunahoo, business manager, Committee for Christian Education and
     Publications, PCA

... as well as the several boards, committees, and denominations who have supported this project.

A cooperative project of the

Presbyterian Church in America
Reformed Presbyterian Church of North America

Published by

Crown & Covenant Publications (RPCNA)
7408 Penn Ave.
Pittsburgh, PA 15208-2531
Phone: (412) 241-0436

A song leader's edition of this book (with music) is available. Many other psalmbooks, psalm tapes, and other materials are also available from the publisher. Write or call for a free catalog.

Third Printing 1997

For the *Trinity Psalter* edition, the cover logo and cover design are used by permission of Great Commission Publications, 7001 Peachtree Industrial Blvd. #120, Norcross, GA 30092-3618. The publishers are grateful for their assistance.

ISBN 1-884527-07-8
Printed in U.S.A.
Library of Congress Catalog Card Number: 93-074255

PREFACE

The Book of Psalms for Singing, the Psalmbook of Crown & Covenant Publishers and the Reformed Presbyterian Church of North America, has been the most widely used complete English-language Psalter of the late Twentieth Century. For 20 years it has faithfully served the needs of Psalm-singing congregations. But its size and cost have limited its usefulness for hymnal-using churches. Few congregations have been willing to add a second hymnal-sized and hymnal-priced book to the one they already use.

Early in 1993, a special committee of the Presbyterian Church in America approached representatives of Crown & Covenant to ask them to consider producing an abridged version of *The Book of Psalms for Singing* that might serve the needs of such congregations: inexpensive enough to be affordable and thin enough to fit in the pew rack together with a hymnal.

This volume represents the fruit of their discussions. While still retaining every verse of all 150 Psalms, this psalter is only one-quarter the size of *The Book of Psalms for Singing*. This drastic reduction was accomplished by generally applying the following guidelines:

1. Using only one *version* of each Psalm (eliminating multiple versions);
2. Recommending only one *tune* for each Psalm (eliminating multiple settings);
3. Providing the *words* only (eliminating musical score).

The resulting thin and inexpensive edition is a joint publishing venture of the PCA and Crown & Covenant, and is warmly commended to the congregations we serve. The words, unless otherwise noted, are under the copyright of Crown and Covenant Publications, and may not be reproduced without permission. For Psalms 48 and 89, permission must be sought from *The Complete Book of Psalms for Singing* (copyright © 1991 by Rowland S. Ward, 358 Mountain Highway, Wantirna, Victoria 3152, Australia).

WHY THE PSALMS?

WHY THE PSALMS? Rather than asking that question, the real question should be, "Why not the Psalms?" Most Christian traditions hold to a high view of Biblical authority. Conservative Christians proclaim the doctrine of Biblical inerrancy. Scripture study and memorization are eagerly encouraged. How can it be that the Psalms, which God gave to His people specifically *to be sung* and which for generations were sung among all the major Protestant groups, are almost universally neglected? How has it happened that the Psalms, which undeniably are the very word of God, have been completely supplanted by hymns in our day?

Let's look at the question from another angle. Should one's reading priority be good Christian literature or the Bible? "Oh, that's easy to answer," you say. While the reading of good Christian literature is profitable and good and should be encouraged, it should never be allowed to replace the greater good of Bible reading, the ultimate source material upon which good Christian books are based. Case is closed. Yet this is precisely what has happened in the area of the church's songs.

What should be the priority in singing? Isn't it self-evident that even the best hymns are nevertheless of human composition and should never be allowed to replace the greater good of Psalm-singing? That this obvious truth has nearly completely "slipped the mind" of the modern church is yet another sign that things are seriously amiss in the worship of our churches. This work is designed to make the metrical Psalms accessible to hymnal-using congregations in a form that is simple and inexpensive.

Old Paths Made New

Perhaps a little more background may help. That the Biblical Book of Psalms was the hymnbook of Israel cannot be doubted. From the time of David to the time of Christ the people of God learned to express their praise of God through the singing of Psalms. While this is universally understood to be true of the Old Testament church, it is seldom recognized that the Psalter has served as the primary hymnal of the New Testament church throughout most of its history.

Consider the evidence. When Jesus and the disciples sang a "hymn" at their Passover observance, the Last Supper, it was likely the Hallel section of the Psalter (consisting of Psalms 113-118) that was sung (Matt. 26:30; Mark 14:26). When the early church "lifted their voices to God with one accord," it was to the words of the 146th and 2nd Psalms (Acts 4:24ff). The church at Corinth sang Psalms (1 Cor. 14:15,26), and Paul commended the singing of "psalms, hymns, and spiritual songs" (Eph. 5:19; Col. 3:16). Whatever one makes of "hymns" and "spiritual songs" (some argue that these are the Psalm titles used in the Septuagint, the Greek version of the Old Testament), the singing of the canonical book of Psalms is encouraged, even commanded. James asks, "Is anyone cheerful? Let him sing psalms" (Greek = *psalleto*, Jas. 5:13). There can be no question that the Apostolic church sang the Psalms. By precept and example Psalm-singing is mandated in the New Testament.

Among the church Fathers, Tertullian (Second Century) and Jerome (mid-Fourth to Fifth Centuries) testify that Psalm-singing was an essential feature of the worship of their day. The singing of Psalms received the strongest commendation from Chrysostom and Augustine. The Fifth Century marks the beginning of the

"Dark Ages," and the onset of a number of ecclesiastical developments regretted by Protestants. Among these was the disappearance of congregational song. Singing became the sole preserve of the monasteries. Yet even then it was the Psalms that the monks read and sang with an almost fanatical zeal. For a thousand years the Psalms inspired the monastic orders. The Reformation of the Sixteenth Century then revived the *congregational* singing of the Psalter, which dominated the church-music scene until the middle of the last century.

Why, then, should we sing the Psalms? John Calvin, the man most responsible for their Sixteenth Century revival, summarizes the answer as well as anyone. Whenever we might look for suitable songs of praise, he says, "we shall not find better songs nor more fitting for the purpose, than the Psalms of David, which the Holy Spirit spoke and made through him...when we sing them, we are certain that God puts in our mouths these, as if He Himself were singing in us to exalt His glory" (*Preface To the Psalter,* 1543).

Few people realize that the Reformed and Presbyterian Churches were exclusively Psalm singing for over 200 years, as were their independent brethren, the Congregationalists and Baptists. Few people realize that the metrical Psalms crossed the Atlantic on the Mayflower (the old *Ainsworth Psalter*), were sung by Sir Francis Drake to the Indians in California (from the *Sternhold and Hopkins Psalter*), and that the first book published in North America was—you guessed it— a Psalter. The enormously popular *Bay Psalm Book* (1640) was the hymnal of American Puritanism, undergoing 70 printings through 1773. When the *Bay Psalm Book* and the favorite among Scotch Irish immigrants, the *Scottish Psalter* (1650) were finally superseded, it was by a book that purported to be yet another Psalter, Isaac Watts' *The Psalms of David Imitated* (1719), from which we get the "hymns" "O God Our Help in Ages Past" (Psalm 90), "Joy to the World" (Psalm 98), and "Jesus Shall Reign" (Psalm 72). It was not until the middle of the last century that hymns began to overtake the Psalms in popular use. Our forefathers, both evangelical and American, were Psalm-singers!

A Stronger Spirituality

All this is well and good, even reassuring for those who respect the tradition of the church. But our chief concern is with the worship and piety of God's people today. Are there any practical benefits that come from Psalm-singing? Indeed there are. It is our conviction that the revival of the Psalms is crucial if the Christian church is ever to regain the strong, Biblical spirituality of the Reformation era.

Louis Benson, the outstanding hymnologist of a previous generation, argued that the *Genevan Psalter* played a vital role in the spread of the Genevan doctrines as well as shaping the piety of the Reformed churches. "The singing of Psalms became the Reformed cultus, the characteristic note distinguishing its worship from that of the Roman Catholic Church," he wrote. Moreover,

> The familiar use of Psalms in worship only emphasized the power of their appeal to the individual experience, and made Psalmody as much a part of the daily life as of public worship. The family in the home, men and women at their daily tasks, were recognized as Huguenots because they were heard singing Psalms. The Psalter became to them the manual of the spiritual life. It ingrained its own characteristics deep in the Huguenot character, and had a great part in making it what it was...to the Huguenot, called to fight and suffer for his principles, the habit of Psalm singing was a providential preparation. The Psalms were his confidence

and strength in quiet and solitude, his refuge from oppression; in the wars of religion they became the songs of the camp and the march, the inspiration of the battle and the consolation in death, whether on the field or at the martyrs stake. It is not possible to conceive of the history of the Reformation in France in such a way that Psalm singing should not have a great place in it (*Journal of the Presbyterian Historical Society*, "John Calvin and the Psalmody of the Reformed Churches," vol. V, June 1909, p. 73).

Thus a distinctive piety develops as a result of Psalm-singing, a strong, militant, and bold spirituality. Calvinism produced what Roland Bainton called "a race of heroes," and Psalm-singing had no small part in bringing this about. These are the songs of the *church militant*. The Huguenots in their struggle against the French monarch, the Dutch in their fight for independence from the Spanish Empire, and the Parliamentary armies in their civil war against the Stuart monarchy all sang the Psalms into battle, often against overwhelming odds. The 68th, "Let God arise," is known as the battle Psalm of the Huguenots. Our Reformed forefather's favorite metaphor for the Christian life was that of warfare. Nearly every Psalm refers to the conflict between the righteous and the wicked (148 of 150 by one count), a theme which is almost nonexistent in modern hymns. One author has said, "When iron was in men's souls, and they needed it in their blood, they sang Psalms." The Psalms will stiffen a church accustomed to accommodation and compromise with the world.

The Psalms, as Benson notes, are also the songs of the *suffering church*. Whenever in the midst of persecution, death, physical illness, depression, or spiritual "desertions" (as the Puritans called them), the people of God have found unparalleled "refuge and strength" in the God of the Psalms.

At the same time, the "songs of Scripture" are the hymns of the *church triumphant*. They inspire the church to believe in the ultimate triumph of its cause. Be encouraged, the Psalms tell us! The nations shall praise our God (e.g., Psalms 47, 66, 67, 100). Christ is upon His throne, ruling with a rod of iron (Psalms 2, 16, 110). Nowhere in Scripture will we find a clearer vision of the triumph of the Gospel. As the church in America finds itself more and more in a hostile environment, it is indeed "of the Lord" that the congregational singing of the Psalms be revived.

Biblical Wholeness

Thus, the Psalms are unrivaled as a complete guide of spiritual life—precisely what they were meant to be. In them we find the whole range of human emotions and experiences. The Psalms are authentic. The joy of praise, the pain of persecution, the comfort of sonship, the sorrow of death, the hope of heaven, and the cry for justice all find full expression, often with vivid realism. This is to say that the Psalms are *human* in a way that few hymns dare to be. The whole body of Christian doctrine and experience is to be found in the Psalms. They are virtually a "little Bible" as Luther called them.

What about the gospel? Showing the profound insight that we regularly expect from him, Luther says the Book of Psalms "should be precious and dear to us if only because it most clearly promises the death and resurrection of Christ, and describes His kingdom, and the nature and standing of all Christian people" (*Preface to the Psalms*, 1528). Likewise Augustine believed, "the voice of Christ and

His Church is well-nigh the only voice to be heard in the Psalms." The time has come to bring them back into the mainstream. A revival of Psalm-singing can only add depth to the shallow waters of contemporary Christianity.

GUIDES TO USING THIS BOOK

A "words-only" edition of the Psalms may seem an oddity at first, but it should be remembered that the use of hymnbooks with music is a relative novelty before the late 19th Century. Most hymnals before this century were "words-only," and even today those found in the churches of Britain and Europe are usually of this type. By one estimate only 10% of a given congregation can read music anyway. We are confident that you will find that most people will adjust quickly to this approach and soon be singing heartily.

Moreover, we think that there are two advantages this format. The first advantage is practical—money. A words-only version can be placed in the pew alongside a hymnal for a relatively inexpensive price. The second advantage is comprehension. Printing the words consecutively allows one to look at the Psalm as a whole and see the progression of its thought. This contrasts sharply with a format which staggers each line of the Psalm within the musical score. You will "feel" like you are singing the word of God rather than just another hymn, and in feeling this sense its authority.

Tunes and Meters

We have attempted to follow the old Reformed ideal of providing a distinctive tune for each Psalm, so that the words and the music become associated with one another. Beneath the words of each Psalm is listed a recommended tune and its meter. For example, Psalm 97 is followed by:

TUNE: ST. ANNE CM (37A)
"O God our help in ages past"

This means that the tune name is St. Anne, its meter is CM, or common meter (8686), and the familiar hymn with which it is usually associated is "O God our help in ages past." The number within the brackets (37A) refers to the page in *The Book of Psalms for Singing* (TBOPFS) where the musical score for St. Anne can be found. For the 30 tunes not found in TBOPFS, one of four hymnals is referenced. They are:

The Hymnbook (1955)
The old *Trinity Hymnal* (1961)
The new *Trinity Hymnal* (1990)
The *Psalter Hymnal* (1987)

In addition, you will find the alphabetical index of tunes in the back with accompanying page references indicating where the tunes can be found in the new *Trinity Hymnal.*

What is meter? Meter is the number of beats, notes, and syllables in a line. Here is the tune St. Anne again to the familiar words of Isaac Watts:

O\God\our\help\in\a\ges\past = 8
Our\hope\for\years\to\come = 6
Our\shel\ter\from\the\stor\my\blast = 8
And\our\e\ter\nal\home = 6

Thus St. Anne is a tune with 8.6.8.6. or "common" meter.

The named meters are:

SM - Short Meter - 6686
SMD - Short Meter Doubled - 6686.6686
CM - Common Meter - 8686
CMD - Common Meter Doubled - 8686.8686
LM - Long Meter - 8888
LMD - Long Meter Doubled - 8888.8888

The numerous unnamed meters are listed in the index in the back. Again, each number represents the number of beats in a line. Here's one more example. Look at Psalm 5. It says,

TUNE: ABERYSTWYTH 7777D (5B)
("Jesus Lover of My Soul")

Each line of this Psalm will have seven beats\notes\syllables:

O\Je\ho\vah\hear\my\words = 7
To\my\thoughts\at\ten\tive\be = 7
Hear\my\cry\my\King\my\God = 7
For\I\make\my\prayer\to\Thee = 7
With\the\morn\ing\light\O\Lord = 7
Thou\shalt\hear\my\voice\and\cry = 7
In\the\morn\my\prayer\ar\range = 7
And\keep\con\stant\watch\will\I = 7

While we would like you to follow our suggestions in the use of tunes so that a body of beloved Psalmody develops, it is possible to substitute any tune with the same meter for the one recommended.

Sources

Finally, at the bottom of the Psalm is listed the source of its words. The main source for the words (134 of 150) is *The Book of Psalms for Singing,* © 1973. When we departed from that book it was for the sake of finding versions in meters for which we had outstanding tunes. Our sources were The United Presbyterian *Book of Psalms,* 1871, from which we used eight versions, the *Irish Psalter,* 1880, from which we used five versions, *The Complete Book of Psalms for Singing,* 1991, from which we used two versions, *The Psalter* (1912), from which we used one, and *The Book of Psalms with Music,* 1950, from which we used parts of Psalm 119.

You will notice that for nearly half of the Psalms there is a secondary source reference. For example, Psalm 6 reads,

Based on *Scottish Psalter,* 1650.

This means that our primary source was TBOPFS, but we found substantial dependence on the Scottish version. Look at Psalm 8 and you'll see another type of reference. It reads,

Elements from *The Psalter,* 1912.

This means that once again our primary source was TBOPFS, but we found *traces* of the 1912 version. We pursued this information because we thought it important to demonstrate that current Psalmody maintains continuity with the older traditions. Over one-fifth of this psalter may be traced to the *Scottish Psalter,* and over one-third to the revisions of the late Nineteenth and early Twentieth Centuries (the 1871, 1880, and 1912 versions). Thus over 60% of this volume is rooted in older Psalters. While much of the language has been updated and many new versions written, (nearly 50% have been completely modernized, dropping the use of old English pronouns and endings), we can be confident that often we are singing the Psalms as our fathers did generations ago. The sources we have been able to trace are as follows:

Scottish Psalter, 1564
Scottish Psalter, 1650
Isaac Watts' *The Psalms of David Imitated,* 1719
The United Presbyterian *Book of Psalms,* 1871
Irish Psalter, 1880
The Psalter, 1912
Bible Songs, 1931
The Book of Psalms with Music, 1950
The Book of Psalms for Singing, 1973
The Complete Book of Psalms for Singing, 1991

When one adds to the above the fact that several of the Genevan settings have been preserved and Genevan tunes used (e.g. Old Hundredth with Psalm 100, Old 124th with Psalm 124, Old 110th with Psalm 129, Old 134th with Psalm 93, Toulon with Psalm 7), the whole tradition of Reformed Psalm singing is represented in this collection.

Getting Started
The typical practice in Calvin's Geneva and among the Huguenots was to sing through the Psalms consecutively, beginning with Psalm 1 and ending with Psalm 150, and then starting over again. This approach has its merits, but is not recom-

mended for congregations for which Psalm singing will be new.

We recommend that you begin by using familiar tunes and familiar Psalms. Start with music that is well known to your congregation, and start with Psalms that are known and beloved. We recommend the following for beginners: Psalms 1, 5, 15, 23, 32, 37, 42, 48, 51, 63, 65, 67, 73, 90, 91, 92, 94, 96, 97, 100, 103, 110, 117, 121, 122, 128, 130, 133, 139, 145, 146. Consult the indices in the back for other tunes that may be familiar to your congregation. Once having learned these, move on to those less familiar.

We would also like to recommend a variety of uses for the Psalms. In addition to singing whole Psalms, they function wonderfully in the following roles:

Calls to worship—e.g., Pss. 8:1,2; 15:1,2; 19:1,2; 24:1,2; 33:1-3; 34:1-3; 47:1; 48:1; etc.
Calls to confession of sin—e.g., Pss. 25:11; 32:1-2, 3-5; 51:1-2, 3-6, 9-11, etc.
Responses (concluding worship)—e.g., Pss. 1:1-2; 3:3,4,8; 5:11,12; 13:5,6; 23:6; 25:4,5; etc.

Intrigued? Then let us get on with singing them. After all, the final proof of the pudding is in the eating, and we are confident that if you once "eat" them, you will never again settle for less.

—*Special Committee on Psalm Singing*
Presbyterian Church in America

Psalm 1

1 O greatly bless-ed is the man
  Who walketh not astray
  In counsel of ungodly men,
  Nor stands in sinners' way,

2 Nor sitteth in the scorner's chair,
  But placeth his delight
  Upon GOD's law, and meditates
  On His law day and night.

3 He shall be like a tree that grows
  Set by the water side,
  Which in its season yields its fruit,
  And green its leaves abide;

  And all he does shall
    prosper well.
4 The wicked are not so,
  But are like chaff which
    by the wind
  Is driven to and fro.

5 In judgment therefore shall
    not stand
  Such as ungodly are,
  Nor in th'assembly of the just
  Shall wicked men appear.

6 Because the way of godly men
  Is to Jehovah known,
  Whereas the way of wicked men
  Shall quite be overthrown.

TUNE: ARLINGTON CM (1A)
("This is The Day the Lord Has Made")

Psalm 2

1 Why do heathen nations rage?
  Why do peoples folly mind?
2 Kings of earth in plots engage,
  Rulers are in league combined;
  Then against Jehovah high,
  And against Messiah's sway,
3 "Let us break their bands,"
    they cry,
  "Let us cast their cords away."

4 But the Lord will scorn them all;
  He will laugh Who sits on high,
5 Then His wrath will on them fall;
  Sore displeased He will reply:
6 "Yet according to My will
  I have set My King to reign,
  And on Zion's holy hill
  My Anointed I'll maintain."

7 His decree I will make known:
  Unto Me the LORD did say,
  "Thou art My be-lov-ed Son;
  I've begotten Thee this day.
8 Ask of Me, and Thee I'll make
  Heir to earth and nations all;
9 Them with iron Thou shalt break,
  Dashing them in pieces small."

10 Therefore, kings, be wise,
    give ear;
  Hearken, judges of the earth;
11 Serve the LORD with godly fear;
  Mingle trembling with your mirth.
12 Kiss the Son, His wrath to turn,
  Lest ye perish in the way,
  For His anger soon will burn.
  Blessed are all that on Him stay.

TUNE: HINTZE 7.7.7.7.D (2) or
SPANISH HYMN (*The Hymnbook,* p. 253)
("How I Love Thy Law, O Lord")

Based on the *Book of Psalms,* 1871 and
The Psalter, 1912

Psalm 3

1 O LORD, how are my foes
　　increased!
　Against me many rise.
2 How many say, "In vain for help
　He on his God relies!"

3 You are my shield and glory,
　　LORD;
　You lifted up my head.
4 I cried out, "LORD!" and from
　　His hill
　To me His answer sped.

5 I lay down, slept, and woke again
　The LORD is keeping me.
6 I will not fear ten thousand men
　Entrenched surrounding me.

7 Arise, O LORD! Save me, my God!
　You punish all my foes.
　You smite the face of
　　wicked men,
　Their teeth break with
　　your blows.

8 Deliverance is from the LORD,
　Salvation His alone!
　O let Your blessing evermore
　Be on Your people shown!

TUNE: NEW BRITAIN CM (3)
("Amazing Grace")

Based on *Scottish Psalter,* 1650

Psalm 4

1 Answer when I call,
　　O God who justifies.
　In my stress You freed me;
　　hear in grace my cries.
2 Sons of men, how long will
　　you my glory shame?
　Will you love what's worthless?
　　Will lies be your aim?

3 Know the LORD His saints has
　　set apart in grace,
　And the LORD will hear me
　　when I seek His face.
4 Tremble in your anger,
　　yet from sin depart.
　On your bed in silence
　　speak within your heart.

5 May you sacrifice now
　　sacrifices just.
　In Jehovah only
　　placing all your trust.
6 "Who will show us goodness?"
　　many people say;
　The light of Your face, LORD,
　　lift on us, we pray.

7 You have given my heart
　　greater joy by far
　Than when grain and new wine
　　most abundant are.
8 So in peace I lie down;
　　I will rest and sleep,
　For, O LORD, You only
　　will me safely keep.

TUNE: PENITENCE 11.11.11.11. (4B)
("In the Hour of Trial")

2

Psalm 5

1 O Jehovah, hear my words;
   To my thoughts attentive be.
2 Hear my cry, my King, my God,
   For I make my prayer to Thee.
3 With the morning light, O LORD,
   Thou shalt hear my voice and cry;
   In the morn my prayer arrange
   And keep constant watch will I.

4 Truly Thou art not a God
   That in sin doth take delight;
   Evil shall not dwell with Thee,
5 Nor the proud stand in Thy sight.
   Evildoers Thou dost hate;
6 Liars Thou wilt bring to naught.
   GOD abhors the man who loves
   Deed of blood or lying thought.

7 But in Thine abundant grace
   To Thy house will I repair;
   Looking to Thy holy place,
   In Thy fear I'll worship there.
8 Since, O LORD, mine enemies
   For my soul do lie in wait,
   Lead me in Thy righteousness;
   Make Thy way before me straight.

9 For they flatter with their tongue;
   In their mouth no truth is found;
   Like an open grave their throat;
   All their thoughts with sin abound.
10 Hold them guilty, O my God;
   Them for all their sins expel;
   Let them fall by their own craft,
   For against Thee they rebel.

11 But let all that trust Thy care
   Ever glad and joyful be;
   Let them joy who love Thy name,
   For they guarded are by Thee.
12 And a blessing rich, O LORD,
   To the righteous Thou wilt yield;
   Thou wilt compass him about
   With Thy favor as a shield.

TUNE: ABERYSTWYTH 7.7.7.7.D (5B)
("Jesus Lover of My Soul")

Based on the *Book of Psalms*, 1871 and
The Psalter, 1912

Psalm 6

1 In anger, LORD, do not rebuke,
   Nor judgment in Your
      wrath decide.
2 My weakness, LORD, pity and heal,
   For in my bones I'm terrified.
3 My soul is in me terrified.
   O LORD, and yet how long
      You take!
4 Return, O LORD; my soul set free,
   And save me for Your
      mercies' sake.

5 For none can remember in death,
   Or there shall your memory keep,
   And who can give You
      praises then,
   Within the confines of the deep.
6 My groaning all day wearies me,
   Through ev'ry night till
      morn appears.
   My grieving makes my bed
      to swim
   And waters all my cot with tears.

7 Because of my enemies all
   This grief is consuming my eyes.
8 Then let evil men all depart!
   The LORD has heard my
      weeping cries.
9 The LORD hears my suppliant cries.
   The LORD has my prayers brought
      to mind.
10 My foes shall be vexed
      and ashamed,
   And sudden shame they all
      will find.

TUNE: TREWEN LMD
(new *Trinity Hymnal*, p. 463)
("A Debtor to Mercy Alone") or
OLIVE'S BROW LM (6)

Based on *Scottish Psalter*, 1650

3

Psalm 7

Verses 1–8

1 O LORD my God, in You
   I refuge take.
  O save me from all those
   who me pursue.
2 Lest he should like a lion
   tear my soul
  And drag me off, with none
   to rescue me.

3 O LORD my God, if wrong is
   in my hands,
4 If I did evil to my friend or foe,
5 Let my pursuer overtake me now
  And trample in the dust my life,
   my soul.

6 Arise, O LORD! In anger
   lift yourself
  Against the fury of my enemies.
  Awake for me! Your judgment
   You have set.
7 Let peoples in assembly
   compass You.

  In triumph over them return
   on high.
8 The LORD now sits to judge the
   peoples all.
  O vindicate me, LORD,
   in righteousness,
  According to integrity in me.

Verses 9–17

9 O let the evil of the wicked cease,
  But every righteous one
   establish firm,
  For You it is Who tries the minds
   and hearts;
  O Righteous God, You are the
   Judge of men.

10 My shield and my defense is
   found with God,
  For He it is Who saves the
   right in heart.

11 A righteous judge, God judges
   righteously,
  And God is filled with anger
   ev'ry day.

12 If one does not repent, God whets
   His sword;
  He has His bow already strung
   and bent.
13 He has prepared His instruments
   of death;
  He makes His arrows fiery,
   deadly shafts.

14 See how the wicked evil thoughts
   conceives,
  Is pregnant with ill will, and
   brings forth lies.
15 He digs a pit, but stumbles in
   himself;
16 On his own head his plotted
   malice falls.

17 I will give thanks to Him
   Who is the LORD
  According to His perfect
   righteousness:
  And I will sing with psalms
   for evermore
  The name of Him Who is the
   LORD Most High.

  TUNE: TOULON 10.10.10.10.
  (new *Trinity Hymnal*, p. 169)
  ("I Greet Thee, Who My Sure
   Redeemer Art")

Psalm 8

1 LORD, our Lord, in all the earth
How excellent Your name!
You above the heav'ns have set
The splendor of Your fame.
2 From the mouths of infants young
You the power of praise compose
In the face of enemies
To stop avenging foes.

3 When I view the skies above
Which Your own fingers made,
When I see the moon and stars
Which You in order laid,
4 What is man so frail and weak
That You should remember him?
What can be the son of man
That You should care for him?

5 Next to God You have made man,
With light and honor crowned.
6 You placed him above
    Your works;
Beneath him all is found:
7 Oxen, sheep, and all wild beasts,
8 Birds, and fish the oceans claim.
9 LORD, our Lord, in all the earth
How excellent Your name!

TUNE: AMSTERDAM 76.76.77.76. (8B)

Elements from *The Psalter*, 1912

Psalm 9

Verses 1–10

1 I now will give wholehearted
    thanks to the LORD,
And all of Your marvelous
    works will record.
2 In You will be glad and
    exultingly cry,
And praise to Your name will
    I sing, O Most High.

3 When backward my foes were all
    turned in despair,
They stumbled and perished
    because You were there.
4 For You have defended my
    judgment and cause;
You sat in just judgment
    upholding Your laws.

5 You chided the nations,
    the wicked destroyed;
Their names You erased and
    forever made void.
6 The foe is consumed, is
    completely erased,
Their cities destroyed and their
    mem'ry effaced.

7 The LORD will eternally
    sit on His throne,
Establishing it for
    His judgment alone.
8 In righteousness He'll judge
    the world from His seat
And unto all peoples
    shall equity mete.

9 The LORD is a stronghold,
    a lofty strong tower,
For all the oppressed in their
    troubles' dark hour.
10 Those knowing Your name, LORD,
    trust You for Your grace;
You have not forsaken those
    seeking Your face.

(Turn page for next section)

11 Sing praise to the LORD, Who in
    Zion does dwell;
  Among all the peoples His
    great doings tell.
12 When blood He avenges,
    His mem'ry is clear;
  The cry of the poor never
    fades from His ear.

13 LORD, see what I suffer from
    malice and hate;
  Have mercy! O lift me
    away from death's gate,
14 That I with the daughter of
    Zion may voice
  Your praises, and in Your
    salvation rejoice.

15 The nations are sunk in the
    pit they prepared;
  Their foot in the net which they
    hid is ensnared.
16 The LORD by His judgment has
    made Himself known,
  He by their own works has the
    wicked o'erthrown.

17 The wicked to death's dark
    abode shall be brought,
  And all of the nations who
    God have forgot.
18 Forgotten no longer the
    cause of the weak,
  Nor perished forever the
    hope of the meek.

19 Rise, LORD, that mere man may not
    make himself strong;
  Let nations be judged in Your
    presence for wrong.
20 Strike terror within them,
    O LORD; always then
  Let nations know truly that
    they are mere men.

    TUNE: JOANNA 11.11.11.11. (9B)
      ("Immortal, Invisible")

    Elements from *The Psalter*, 1912

Psalm 10

Verses 1–11

1 Why do You stand so far away,
    O LORD?
  Why do You hide Yourself in
    troublous times?
2 In arrogance the wicked trap
    the poor;
  Let them be caught in schemes
    they have devised.

3 The wicked boasts about his
    heart's desires;
  The covetous renounces, spurns
    the LORD.
4 In pride the wicked see no need
    to seek;
  In all his thoughts he says,
    "There is no God."

5 He's self–assured, Your judgments
    far from him.
  At all his foes he only puffs
    in scorn.
6 In heart he thinks, "I never shall
    be moved;
  Through ages all no evil shall
    I meet."

7 His mouth is filled with oaths and
    lies and threats:
  Beneath his tongue are evil
    thoughts and deeds.
8 He sits in ambush 'mid the
    village homes;
  The innocent he murders secretly.

  In stealth he watches for some
    hapless one.
9 He like a lion crouches in his den.
  He hides himself that he may
    seize the poor;
  To seize the poor he traps him
    in his net.

10 The hapless one he crushes,
    tramples down,
  When he has made him fall
    beneath his might.

11 In heart he thinks, "God has
    forgotten this;
    He hid His face, so He will
    never see."

Verses 12–18

12 Arise, O Lord! O God, lift up
    Your hand!
    Forget not those who have
    afflicted been.
13 Why does the wicked proudly
    scoff at God
    And say in heart, "He'll never
    take account"?

14 You see! You note disorder
    and distress.
    That You may take it all into
    Your hands.
    The hapless may commit
    himself to You;
    You are the helper of the
    fatherless.

15 O break the wicked,
    evildoer's arm!
    Seek out his wickedness till
    You find none.
16 The Lord is king through
    all eternity;
    The heathen nations perish
    from His land.

17 You hear, O Lord, the longing
    of the meek;
    Their heart You strengthen;
    You incline Your ear.
18 Do justice to oppressed
    and fatherless.
    That man of earth may terrify
    no more.

TUNE: PENITENTIA 10.10.10.10.
(10A)

Psalm 11

1 My trust is in the Lord;
    How can you say to me,
    "Now like a bird from peril haste
    And to your mountain flee!
2 The wicked bend the bow
    With arrow fixed for flight,
    And stealthily in darkness go
    The true in heart to smite.

3 "Foundations are destroyed!
    What can the righteous try?"
4 The Lord is in His holy place;
    The Lord's throne is on high.
    His eyes will surely see,
    His eyelids try men's sons.
5 The Lord tries just and
    wicked men;
    His soul hates cruel ones.

6 Upon all wicked men
    He'll rain entangling snares.
    Brimstone and fire and
    burning wind
    He for their cup prepares.
7 For righteous is the Lord,
    And He loves righteousness;
    And every one who upright is
    Will see His gracious face.

TUNE: TERRA BEATA SMD
(new *Trinity Hymnal*, p. 111)
("This Is My Father's World")

Elements from the *Book of Psalms, 1871*
and *Bible Songs*, 1931

Psalm 12

1 O Thou, Jehovah, grant us help,
  Because the godly cease;
  And from among the sons of men
  The faithful now decrease.

2 And to his neighbor every one
  Doth utter vanity;
  They with a double heart
      do speak
  And lips of flattery.

3 The LORD will cut off all false lips,
  Tongues that speak proudly thus:
4 "We'll with our tongue prevail;
      our lips
  Are ours; who's lord o'er us?"

5 "Because the poor are
      sorely pressed,
  Because the needy sighs,
  To give the safety they desire,"
  The LORD says, "I'll arise."

6 Jehovah's words are words
      most pure;
  They are like silver tried
  In earthen furnace, seven times
  That has been purified.

7 LORD, Thou shalt them
      preserve and keep
8 Forever from this race.
  On ev'ry side the wicked walk,
  With vile men high in place.

TUNE: BELMONT CM (12A)
("The Spirit Breathes Upon the Word")
("How Precious Is the Book Divine")

Based on *Scottish Psalter,* 1650

Psalm 13

1 How long wilt Thou forget me?
  Shall it forever be?
  O LORD, how long neglect me,
  And hide Thy face from me
2 How long my soul take counsel,
  Thus sad in heart each day?
  How long shall foes exulting,
  Subject me to their sway?

3 O LORD, my God, consider,
  And hear my earnest cries;
  Lest I in death should slumber,
  Enlighten Thou mine eyes:
4 Lest foes be heard exclaiming
  Against him we prevailed;
  And they that vex my spirit
  Rejoice when I have failed.

5 But on Thy tender mercy
  I ever have relied;
  With joy in Thy salvation
  My heart shall still confide.
6 And I with voice of singing
  Will praise the LORD alone,
  Because to me His favor
  He has so largely shown.

TUNE: PASSION CHORALE 76.76.D
(new *Trinity Hymnal,* p. 247)
("O Sacred Head Now Wounded")

The *Book of Psalms,* 1871

8

Psalm 14

1 The fool in heart is saying,
"There surely is no God."
Corrupt and vile their deeds are;
Not one of them does good.
2 The LORD looks down
from heaven
On sons of men abroad
To see which one has wisdom,
If any seeks for God.

3 All far astray have wandered;
They all to vileness run.
Not one of them is righteous,
No, not a single one.
4 Have they of truth no knowledge,
These evilworkers all,
Who eat like bread my people
And on GOD do not call?

5 There shall they be in terror
For God is with the just;
6 You would confound
one struggling;
Jehovah is his trust.
7 Salvation out of Zion
Who will to Isr'el bring?
The LORD brings back His captives.
Joy, Jacob! Isr'el, sing!

TUNE: MUNICH 76.76.D
(new *Trinity Hymnal*, p. 140)
("O Word of God Incarnate")

Psalm 15

1 LORD, in Thy tent who will
Abide with Thee,
And on Thy holy hill
A dweller be?
2 Who walks in uprightness,
Who worketh righteousness,
Who doth the truth express
Unfeignedly;

3 Whose tongue doth not defame
Nor harm his friend,
Who to his neighbor's shame
No ear doth lend,
4 Who has the vile abhorred
But honor doth accord
To those who fear the LORD
And Him attend.

When to his hurt he swears
Naught changes he;
5 His gold no increase bears
From usury;
His hands no bribes receive
The guiltless to aggrieve.
Lo, he who thus doth live
Unmoved shall be.

TUNE: LOWRY 64.64.66.64. (15)
("Savior, Thy Dying Love")

Psalm 16

1 Preserve me, O my God;
  I put my trust in You.
  LORD, I confess, You are my Lord;
  No good have I but You.
2 The godly ones on earth,
  Those holy in Your sight,
3 The noble and majestic ones,
  Fill me with great delight.

4 Their sorrows multiply
  Who after idols seek.
  To them I'll no blood off'rings make;
  Their names I'll never speak.
5 The LORD the portion is
  Of my inheritance.
  He fills my cup, my lot prepares,
  Secures to me His grants.

6 The lines that fell to me
  Enclose a pleasant site.
  The heritage that I received
  To me is a delight.
7 I bless the LORD Who guides
  With counsel that is right.
  My heart within me He directs
  To teach me in the night.

8 I always keep the LORD
  Before me, Him to see.
  Because He is at my right hand
  I never moved shall be.
9 Thus gladness fills my soul;
  My joy must be expressed
  With my whole being, for my flesh
  Securely finds its rest.

10 My soul You will not leave
  In death's dark pit to be.
  Corruption You will not permit
  Your Holy One to see.
11 The path of life You'll show;
  Of joy You hold great store.
  Before Your face, at Your right hand,
  Are pleasures evermore.

TUNE: LEOMINSTER SMD (25A)
("Not What My Hands Have Done")

Based on *Book of Psalms*, 1871, and Psalm
16A, *The Book of Psalms for Singing*, 1973;
altered 1994

Psalm 17

Verses 1–7

1 Give ear to what is right, O LORD!
  O listen to my cry!
  Give heed to this my
      earnest prayer
  From lips which do not lie.
2 May judgment from Your
      presence come
  Which will me vindicate,
  And always may Your
      searching eyes
  See what is just and straight.

3 For You have scrutinized my heart;
  You came to me by night.
  You've probed and found
      no ill intent;
  My mouth speaks only right.
4 From acts of men, from violence,
  I'm guarded by Your word;
5 My steps held closely to Your paths;
  My footsteps have not erred.

6 On You, O God, my soul
      has called,
  For You will answer me.
  O listen to my earnest words!
  Incline Your ear to me!
7 In wondrous ways You
      mercy show,
  O You preserving those
  Who seek to find at Your
      right hand
  A refuge from their foes.

Verses 8–15

8 Keep me the pupil of Your eye;
  Beneath Your wings me hide
9 From wicked men and
      deadly foes
  Who press on every side.
10 They are enclosed in their
      own fat;
  Their boasting words abound.
11 They compass us and fix
      their eyes
  To cast us to the ground.

10

12 My enemy's a lion strong
   That craves to tear his prey.
   He's like a lion young that lurks
   In ambush every day.
13 Arise, O Lord. Confront my foe.
   O bring him very low!
   O save my soul from wicked men!
   Let them feel Your sword's blow.

14 Save me by Your own hand, O
      Lord,
   From worldly men of earth,
   Who only in this present life
   Know anything of worth.
   You filled them with the
      wealth You stored,
   Their children satisfied;
   So they may leave enough behind
   Their young ones to provide.

15 But as for me, with righteousness
   Shall I behold Your face.
   I shall be satisfied to wake
   And see You face to face.

   TUNE: EVAN CM (23A)

Psalm 18

Verses 1–13

1 I love You, Lord! You are
      my strength,
2 The Lord, my rock, my fort,
      my power,
   My God, my hiding place,
      my shield,
   My horn of safety, and my tower.
3 Because He's ever to be praised,
   Unto the Lord I lift my cry;
   For I shall be delivered thus
   From all the foes who me defy.

4 With cords of death on every side,
   I was assailed by floods of sin,
5 Entangled by the grave's
      strong cords,
   My way with snares of death
      hemmed in.

6 In my distress I called the Lord;
   My cry to God for help was clear.
   He from His temple heard
      my voice;
   My cry before Him reached
      His ear.

7 The earth then quivered to
      its depths;
   The mountains rocked with
      trembling frame;
   The whole world's firm
      foundations shook,
   Because He in His anger came.
8 His nostrils smoked; His mouth
      belched fire;
   And glowing coals flamed forth
      from Him.
9 He bent the sky as He
      came down;
   Thick darkness hovered
      under Him.

10 He swiftly on a cherub flew;
   On wings of wind He rushed
      in flight.
11 He hid Himself in darkness deep,
   Thick clouds about Him black
      as night.
12 Then through the clouds His
      brilliance burst
   With lightnings, hailstones,
      coals of fire.
13 The Lord Most High then
      thundered forth;
   He spoke with hailstones,
      coals of fire.

(Turn page for next section)

11

14 The deadly arrows He sent forth
   Dispersed His foes in wild retreat.
   The flaming lightnings He
      shot out
   Made their discomfiture complete.
15 Then channels of the seas
      were seen,
   Laid bare the world's foundations
      vast;
   At Your rebuke, O LORD,
      they shook,
   And at Your nostrils' angry blast.

16 He reached from heav'n and
      rescued me
   From many waters swelling high;
17 From those that hate me
      set me free,
   From foes that stronger
      were than I.
18 In my distress my foes came on;
   The LORD was my security;
19 He brought me forth and
      gave me room,
   Because He took delight in me.

20 According to my righteousness
   I am rewarded by the LORD;
   According as my hands
      were clean,
   He gives to me a just reward.
21 I've kept the pathway of the LORD
   And from my God did not depart,
22 I've kept His judgments in
      my sight,
   His statutes shut not from
      my heart.

23 Sincere toward Him, I set
      my guard
   To keep myself away from sin.
24 My righteousness the LORD
      rewards
   As in His sight my hands
      are clean.
25 To gracious men You gracious
      are;
   The perfect You perfection show;

26 The pure You show that You
      are pure;
   Your cunning will the
      crafty know.

Verses 27–37

27 A humble people You lift up;
   But haughty eyes You
      humble low.
28 You light my lamp and
      make it shine.
   The LORD my God makes
      darkness glow.
29 By You I can attack a troop,
   And by my God I leap a wall.
30 Our God! How perfect is His way!
   No promise of the LORD can fall.

   He is a shield around all those
   Who flee to Him from
      foes abroad.
31 For who is God, except the LORD?
   Who is a rock, except our God?
32 My God girds up my loins
      with strength;
   My way He perfects with
      His hand.
33 He makes my feet swift like
      the doe's;
   On heights triumphant makes
      me stand.

34 My arms can bend a bow of brass;
   Hands trained by Him for
      battle wait.
35 Your gift, my shield! Your hand,
      my help!
   Your gentleness has made
      me great.
36 You for my steps have cleared
      the way;
   My feet slide not while I pursue;
37 I overtake my fleeing foes;
   I turn not till I thrust
      them through.

38 My foes can rise again no more;
They at my feet are fallen now.
39 For You have made me strong
for war;
You've made my foes beneath
me bow.
40 You made them turn their backs
and flee,
That I my haters might destroy.
41 They cried for help, but no
one came;
They begged the Lord; He sent
no joy.

42 I crushed them small as
flying dust;
Like trampled mud I let them fall.
43 You rescued me from
peoples' strife,
Made me the head of nations all.
A people I knew not will serve
44 And, when they hear me,
will obey.
The sons of strangers,
trembling come
45 And from their strongholds
fade away.

46 Jehovah lives! Bless-ed be
my Rock!
The God who saves exalted be!
47 The God Who vengeance
executes,
And humbles nations under me.
48 He saves me from my enemies;
Yes, You will now exalt me far
Above the men of violence
Who risen up against me are.

49 I therefore will give thanks to You
Among the nations all, O Lord;
And I will sing the psalms
of praise,
To Your great name will
praise accord.

He to His king salvation gives,
50 To His anointed show His grace;
His mercy evermore extends
To David and his promised race.

TUNE: SWEET HOUR LMD
(new *Trinity Hymnal,* p. 634)
("Sweet Hour of Prayer")

Psalm 19

Verses 1–6

1 The spacious heav'ns declare
The glory of our God;
The firmament displays
His handiwork abroad;
2 Day unto day doth utter speech,
And night to night doth
knowledge teach.

3 Aloud they do not speak;
They utter forth no word,
Nor into language break;
Their voice is never heard;
4 Yet through the world their
line extends,
Their words to earth's
remotest ends.

In heav'n He set a tent
A dwelling for the sun,
5 Which as a mighty man
Delights his course to run.
He, bridegroomlike in his array,
Comes from his chamber,
bringing day.

6 His daily going forth
Is from the end of heav'n:
The firmament to him
Is for his circuit giv'n;
And everywhere from end to end,
His radiant heat he doth extend.

(Turn page for next section)

7 Jehovah's perfect law
  Restores the soul again;
  His testimony sure
  Gives wisdom unto men;
8 The precepts of the LORD are right,
  And fill the heart with
        great delight.

  The LORD's command is pure,
  Enlightening the eyes;
9 Jehovah's fear is clean,
  More lasting than the skies.
  The judgments of the
        LORD express
  His truth and perfect
        righteousness.

10 They're more to be desired
  Than stores of finest gold;
  Than honey from the comb
  More sweetness far they hold.
11 With warnings they Thy
        servant guard;
  In keeping them is great reward.

12 His errors who can know?
  Cleanse me from hidden stain.
13 Keep me from willful sins,
  Nor let them o'er me reign.
  And then I upright shall appear
  And be from great
        transgression clear.

14 Let all the words I speak
  And all the thoughts within
  Come up before Thy sight
  And Thine approval win.
  O Thou Jehovah, unto me
  My rock and my Redeemer be.

TUNE: COLUMBIA 66.66.88.
(new *Trinity Hymnal*, p. 112)
("Praise Ye, Praise Ye the Lord")

Based on the *Book of Psalms,* 1871 and
      The Psalter, 1912

Psalm 20

1 The LORD in your distress attend;
  Let Jacob's God exalt you still;
2 Help from the holy temple send
  And strengthen you from
        Zion's hill.

3 May He your sacrifice regard,
  And all your off'rings bear
        in mind;
4 May He your heart's
        desire reward,
  Fulfilling all you have designed.

5 In your salvation we'll rejoice,
  In our God's name our
        banners raise.
  O may Jehovah hear your voice,
  Grant all you ask through all
        your days.

6 I know now that the LORD defends
  And saves His own anointed king.
  From holy heav'n He
        answer sends;
  His right hand saving power
        will bring.

7 In char-iots some boast
        confidence,
  And on their horses some rely;
  But we boast only one defense,
  The name of God, the
        LORD Most High.

8 While we are raised and
        upright stand,
  Our foes are made to
        bow and fall.
9 O save the king, LORD,
        by Your hand,
  And answer us the day we call.

TUNE: RETREAT LM (119R)
("From Every Stormy Wind")

Based on the *Book of Psalms,* 1871

14

Psalm 21

1 The king in Thy great strength,
    O LORD,
Shall very joyful be;
And in Thy saving help he shall
Rejoice most fervently.
2 For Thou upon him hast
    bestowed
All that his heart would have;
And Thou from him didst
    not withhold
Whate'er his lips did crave.

3 For Thou wilt meet him with
    Thy gifts
Of blessings manifold,
And Thou hast set upon his head
A crown of purest gold.
4 When he requested life of Thee,
Thou life to him didst give;
Such length of days Thou
    gavest him
He evermore should live.

5 In Thy salvation he is great,
And glorified is he;
And Thou upon him hast bestowed
Most glorious majesty.
6 For Thou wilt ever set on him
The blessings of Thy grace,
And Thou wilt cause him
    to be filled
With joy before Thy face.

7 Because the king trusts in
    the LORD,
Through cov'nant love
    that's proved,
Through grace of Him Who
    is Most High,
The king shall not be moved.
8 Thy hand shall reach to ev'ry man
Who is thine enemy,
And thy right hand shall
    find out all
Who hate thee needlessly.

9 For thou wilt make them
    blaze as fire
In presence of thy power.
The LORD shall swallow them
    in wrath;
The fire shall them devour.
10 Their offspring thou wilt
    strike from earth,
Their seed from sons of men.
11 Their evil plans, their
    cunning plots
Against thee are in vain.

12 For thou wilt make them
    turn their back;
Thou wilt thine arrows place
Upon thy strings, in readiness
To fly against their face.
13 In Thine omnipotence, O LORD,
Exalt Thyself on high;
Then we shall sing;
    with psalms of praise
Thy might we glorify.

TUNE: HETHERTON CMD (48B)
("Majestic Sweetness Sits Enthroned")

Based on *Scottish Psalter*, 1650

Psalm 22

Verses 1–12

1 My God, my God, O why
    have You
Forsaken me? O why
Are You so far from giving help
And from my groaning cry?
2 By day and night, my God, I call;
Your answer still delays.
3 And yet You are the Holy One
Who dwells in Isr'el's praise.

4 Our fathers put their trust in You;
From You their rescue came.
5 They begged You and You set
    them free;
They were not put to shame.
6 But as for me, I am a worm
And not a man at all.
To men I am despised and base;
Their scornings on me fall.

7 All those who look at me
    will laugh
And cast reproach at me.
Their mouths they open wide:
    they wag
Their heads in mockery.
8 "The Lord was his reliance once;
Now see what God will send.
Yes, let God rise and set him free,
This man that was His friend."

9 You took me from my
    mother's womb
To safety at the breast.
10 Since birth when I was cast
    on You
In You, my God, I rest.
11 Be not far off, for grief is near,
And none to help is found;
12 For bulls of Bashan in
    their strength
Now circle me around.

Verses 13–22

13 Their lion jaws they open wide,
And roar to tear their prey.
14 My heart is wax, my bones unknit,
My life is poured away.
15 My strength is only broken clay;
My mouth and tongue are dry,
For in the very dust of death
You there make me to lie.

16 For see how dogs encircle me!
On every side there stands
A brotherhood of cruelty;
They pierce my feet and hands.
17 My bones are plain for me
    to count;
Men see me and they stare.
18 My clothes among them
    they divide,
And gamble for their share.

19 Now hurry, O my Strength,
    to help!
Do not be far, O Lord!
20 But snatch my soul from
    raging dogs,
And spare me from the sword.
21 From lion's mouth and
    oxen's horns
O save me; hear my prayer!
22 And to my brethren in the church
Your name I will declare.

Verses 23–31

23 Let those that fear the Lord
    sing praise!
Give glory to Him now,
All Jacob's seed; all Isr'el's seed,
In awe before Him bow.
24 For He did not despise nor spurn
The grief of one oppressed,
Nor did He shun his cry for help,
But heard and gave him rest.

25 When I proclaim my praise
    of You,
Then all the church will hear,
And I will pay my vows in full
Where men hold Him in fear.

26 The wretched poor will eat
   their fill
And will be made secure.
And those who seek will
   praise the LORD.
So let your hearts endure.

27 Then men remember will the LORD
To earth's remotest shore,
And all the Gentile kindreds turn
To worship and adore.
28 For all dominion in the earth
Is only of the LORD.
Among the nations He controls
The power of the sword.

29 To Him will all the rich
   bow down
Who feast and live in ease.
And all those souls descend
   to dust
Will fall upon their knees.
30 There shall forever be a seed
To serve Him faithfully;
A generation of the LORD
It shall accounted be.

31 And they will come and
   will make known
To people yet to be
The righteousness that is His own,
For none did this but He.

TUNE: HORSLEY CM
(old *Trinity Hymnal*, p. 191)

Psalm 23

1 The LORD's my Shepherd,
   I'll not want;
2 He makes me down to lie
In pastures green; He leadeth me
The quiet waters by.

3 My soul He doth restore again;
And me to walk doth make
Within the paths of righteousness,
Ev'n for His own name's sake.

4 Yea, though I walk in
   death's dark vale,
Yet will I fear no ill;
For Thou art with me, and Thy rod
And staff me comfort still.

5 A table Thou has furnished me
In presence of my foes;
My head Thou dost with
   oil anoint,
And my cup overflows.

6 Goodness and mercy all my life
Shall surely follow me;
And in GOD's house forevermore
My dwelling place shall be.

TUNE: CRIMOND CM (23B)

Based on *Scottish Psalter,* 1650

17

Psalm 24

1 The earth and the riches
    with which it is stored,
The world and its dwellers,
    belong to the LORD.
2 For He on the seas its
    foundation has laid,
And firm on the waters
    it pillars has stayed.

3 O who shall the mount of
    Jehovah ascend?
Or who in the place of
    His holiness stand?
4 The man of pure heart and
    of hands without stain,
Who has not sworn falsely
    nor loved what is vain.

5 He shall from Jehovah
    a blessing receive;
The God of salvation
    shall righteousness give.
6 Thus looking to Him is
    a whole bless-ed race,
All those who, like Jacob,
    are seeking Your face.

7 O gates, lift your heads!
    Ageless doors, lift them high!
The great King of glory
    to enter draws nigh!
8 O who is the King
    that in glory draws near?
The LORD, mighty LORD
    of the battle is here!

9 O gates, lift your heads!
    Ageless doors, lift them high!
The great King of glory
    to enter draws nigh!
10 This great King of glory,
    O Who can He be?
Jehovah of hosts,
    King of glory is He!

TUNE: GREYFRIARS 11.11.11.11. (24C)

Based on the *Book of Psalms*, 1871 and
The Psalter, 1912

Psalm 25

Verses 1–7

1 To Thee I lift my soul,
2 O LORD; I trust in Thee,
My God; let me not be ashamed
Nor foes exult o'er me.
3 Yea, none that wait on Thee
Shall be ashamed at all;
But those that wantonly
    transgress,
Upon them shame shall fall.

4 Show me Thy ways, O LORD;
Thy paths, O teach Thou me,
5 And do Thou lead me
    in Thy truth;
Therein my teacher be.
For Thou art God that dost
To me salvation send,
And I upon Thee all the day
Expecting do attend.

6 Thy tender mercies, LORD,
To mind do Thou recall,
And lovingkindnesses, for they
Have been through ages all.
7 My sins of youth, my faults,
Do Thou, O LORD, forget;
In lovingkindness think on me
And for Thy goodness great.

Verses 8–15

8 The LORD is good and just;
The way He'll sinners show;
9 The meek in judgment
    He will guide
And make His path to know.
10 All pathways of the LORD
Are truth and mercy sure,
To such as keep His covenant
And testimonies pure.

11 Now for Thine own name's sake,
O LORD, I Thee entreat
To pardon my iniquity,
For it is very great.

18

12 Who fears the LORD is taught
The way to understand;
13 His soul shall ever dwell at ease,
His seed possess the land.

14 The secret of the LORD
Shall all who fear Him know;
The knowledge of His covenant
He unto them will show.
15 My eyes upon the LORD
Continually are set;
For He it is that shall bring forth
My feet out of the net.

Verses 16–22

16 O turn to me Thy face;
To me Thy mercy show;
For I am very desolate,
And brought exceeding low.
17 My griefs of heart abound;
My sore distress relieve.
18 See my affliction and my pain,
And all my sins forgive.

19 Consider Thou my foes
Because they many are;
And it a cruel hatred is
Which they against me bear.
20 O do Thou keep my soul;
Do Thou deliver me;
And let me not be put to shame
Because I trust in Thee.

21 Because I wait for Thee
Let truth and right defend;
22 Redemption, Lord, to Is-ra-el
From all his troubles send.

TUNE: TRENTHAM SM (25D)
("Breathe on Me, Breath of God")

Based on *Scottish Psalter,* 1650

Psalm 26

1 Judge me, O LORD,
for I have walked
In my integrity,
And ever with unwav'ring heart
Have trusted, LORD, in Thee.
2 Examine me, and prove me, LORD;
Try heart and mind, I pray.
3 Thy mercy is before my eyes;
Thy truth has led my way.

4 I will not with dissemblers go,
With false men will not wait.
5 I will not sit with wicked men;
Their company I hate.
6 I'll wash my hands in innocence,
Approach Thine altar, LORD,
7 That with a thankful voice I may
Thy wonders all record.

8 The habitation of Thy house,
O LORD, is my delight;
The place in which Thy
glory dwells
Is lovely in my sight.
9 With sinners gather not my soul;
Spare me from blood they spill.
10 In their hand is a wicked scheme;
Their right hand bribes do fill.

11 But as for me, I'll humbly walk
In my integrity.
Redeem Thou me, and in
Thy grace
Be merciful to me.
12 Because my foot is standing now
Upon a level place;
Within the congregation great
Jehovah I will bless.

TUNE: REST CM (95B)

Based on *Scottish Psalter,* 1650

Psalm 27

Verses 1–6

1 The LORD's my shining light
And my salvation sure;
Who can fill me with fright
Or move my heart secure?
The LORD's my stronghold
   ever near;
Of Whom then shall I stand
   in fear?

2 When adversaries came
To eat my flesh away,
Those wicked tripped in shame,
And fell to their dismay.
3 Though hosts surround,
   I will not quail;
And still I trust, though war assail.

4 My one desire has been,
Still to the LORD I'll pray,
That all my days within
The LORD's house I may stay,
The LORD's own beauty to admire,
And in His temple to inquire.

5 When troubles fill my day,
When fears and dangers throng,
Securely hid I'll stay
In His pavilion strong.
He'll hide me in His tent always;
And high upon a rock me raise.

6 My head shall lifted be
Above my enemies.
Within His tent with glee
I'll offer sacrifice.
With shouts of joy my song
   I'll bring;
There praises to the LORD I'll sing.

Verses 7–13

7 LORD, hear me when I cry!
O answer me in grace!
8 Each time I hear You say,
"Enquire and seek my face,"
My heart in glad response
   will speak,
"Your face, O LORD, I'll
   always seek."

9 Hide not Your face from me,
Your servant now, I pray;
The day You angry be
O turn me not away!
You've been my help.
   Forsake me not!
God, my Salvation, leave me not!

10 Though parents may betray,
The LORD will care for me.
11 Teach me, O LORD, Your way;
On level path lead me.
For me my foes in ambush wait;
My way is lined with those
   who hate.

12 O to my foes' desire
Hand me not over now!
They cunningly conspire
Their charges false to vow.
Their every breath is cruelty;
How hopeless seems my cause
   to be!

13 O had I not believed
That I would surely see
The goodness of the LORD
With those that living be!
Wait for the LORD!
   With strength restored,
Be brave in heart.
   Wait for the LORD.

TUNE: ST. JOHN 66.66.88. (27F)
("Within Your Temple, Lord")

Based on *The Psalter*, 1912

20

Psalm 28

1 To Thee, Jehovah, will I cry,
My rock; O, be not silent now!
Lest, if Thou hold Thy peace, I be
Like those who in the pit lie low.
2 O, hear my supplication's voice,
When unto Thee for help I cry,
When to Thy holy oracle
I lift my pleading hands on high.

3 O, with the wicked draw me not
Away, nor with the men of sin;
Who to their neighbors speak
of peace,
But evil is their heart within;
4 Give them according to
their deed,
Their evil doings all reward;
Give them according to
their works,
Return them their desert, O LORD.

5 Since they Jehovah's mighty acts,
And doings of his hands disdain,
He will destroy them in his wrath,
And never build them up again.
6 Blest be Jehovah! He hath heard
My supplication's voice in heav'n.
7 Jehovah is my strength and shield;
I trusted him, He help hath giv'n.

And therefore shall my
heart exult,
My song shall of His praises be.
8 He is their strength;
the saving strength
Of His anointed one is He.
9 O, save the nation of Thy love,
O, bless Thy chosen heritage;
Feed them and lead them
as a flock,
Lift Thou them up from
age to age.

TUNE: TALLIS CANON LM
(new *Trinity Hymnal*, p. 401)
("All Praise to Thee My God This Night")

Irish Psalter, 1880

Psalm 29

1 O give to Jehovah,
you sons of the Mighty,
Both glory and strength
to Jehovah accord!
2 O give to the LORD
His name's greatness of glory!
In splendor of holiness
worship the LORD!

3 The voice of Jehovah
resounds on the waters;
The glorious God
thunders forth from the height.
The LORD is upon the
great sweep of the waters
4 The LORD's voice in splendor!
The LORD's voice in might!

5 The voice of Jehovah
is breaking the cedars!
Jehovah rips Lebanon's
cedars apart!
6 The slopes of Mount Hermon
like calves they are leaping!
And Lebanon's hills
like young antelope start!

7 The voice of Jehovah
divides flames of lightning
And causes the fiery
flashes to break!
8 The voice of the LORD makes
the wilderness tremble;
The LORD makes the desert of
Kadesh to shake!

9 The voice of the LORD makes
the deer twist in labor!
The highstanding forest of trees
it strips bare!
And all of the length and the
breadth of His temple
And all things within it
His glory declare!

(Continues)

21

10 The LORD on His throne sat above
the great deluge!
The LORD on His throne sits as
King without cease!
11 The LORD is the One Who gives
strength to His people!
The LORD is the One Who will
bless them with peace!

TUNE: KREMSER 12.11.12.11. (29A)
("We Gather Together")

Based on the *Book of Psalms*, 1871

Psalm 30

1 O LORD, I will exalt You,
For You have lifted me;
My foes You have allowed not
To glory over me.
2 O LORD my God, I pleaded
That You might heal and save;
3 LORD, You from death
have ransomed
And kept me from the grave.

4 His saints, O praise Jehovah
And thank His holy name.
5 His anger lasts a moment,
His grace a whole life time.
For sorrow, like a pilgrim,
May tarry all the night,
But then a shout of joy comes
When dawns the morning light.

6 In prosp'rous days I boasted,
"Unmoved I shall remain."
7 O LORD, You by Your favor
My mount in strength maintain;
For when Your face was hidden,
I soon was troubled sore.
8 I'll cry to You, Jehovah;
The LORD I will implore.

9 Is there in my blood profit
When in the grave I dwell?
Will dust proclaim Your praises,
Your truth and glory tell?

10 O hear me now, Jehovah!
Be gracious unto me!
To You I cry, Jehovah!
O now my helper be!

11 You now have turned my sorrow
To dancing full of joy;
You loosened all my sackcloth
And girded me with joy.
12 To You sing psalms, my glory,
And never silent be!
O LORD my God, I'll thank You
Through all eternity.

TUNE: ANGEL'S STORY 76.76.D (30A)
("O Jesus I Have Promised")

Based on the *Book of Psalms*, 1871 and
The Psalter, 1912

"O Sacred head"

22

Psalm 31

Verses 1–16

1 In You, Lord, I take refuge;
  Ashamed let me not be.
  Your righteousness eternal
  Express by saving me;
2 Incline Your ear to hear me;
  With speed deliver me.
  To me O be a strong rock
  A fort to rescue me.

3 You are my rock and fortress;
  For Your sake lead and guide.
4 Free me from nets they've hidden;
  My stronghold You abide.
5 I now commit my spirit
  Into Your outstretched hand.
  I know You have redeemed me,
  Lord God of truths that stand.

6 I hate those serving idols;
  My trust is in the Lord.
7 I'll triumph in Your mercy;
  For anguish You regard.
  You've known my soul's
      afflictions,
  Kept me from hostile hand.
8 My feet You have established
  Where they have room to stand.

9 O Lord, have mercy on me,
  For anguish fills my life;
  My eye, my soul, my body
  Are all consumed with grief.
10 My life is drained by sorrow,
  My years with sighing spent;
  I've lost my strength by sinning;
  My bones are weak and bent.

11 To all my foes a byword,
  A dread to those near me,
  A scorn to all my neighbors,
  At sight of me they flee.
12 Like dead men I'm forgotten,
  A broken jar thrown out.
13 I've slanders heard of many,
  And fear is all about.

When foes conspire against me,
  My murder meditate,
14 In You, O Lord, I'm trusting;
  "You are my God," I state.
15 My times are all in Your hand;
  Free me from foes who chase.
16 Your face shine on Your servant;
  O save me in Your grace.

Verses 17–24

17 Let me not be ashamed, Lord,
  Because on You I call.
  Ashamed shall be the wicked,
  As dead men silenced all.
18 All false lips shall be silenced,
  Whose speech is insolent,
  Who boldly blame the righteous
  And proudly show contempt.

19 How great the good You've treasured
  For them who worship You,
  Prepared for those who trust You
  Where sons of men may view.
  You by your presence hide them
20 From all men plotting wrongs;
  You keep them in Your shelter
  Safe from the strife of tongues.

21 The Lord be ever bless-ed,
  For He has made me know
  The mercy and protection
  His city walls bestow.
22 I said when filled with panic,
  "I'm cut off from Your eyes!"
  Yet when to You I called out,
  You heard my pleading cries.

23 O love the Lord, you godly!
  The Lord the faithful keeps.
  But He repays the haughty
  That what he sows he reaps.
24 Be strong! He'll keep refreshing
  Your heart with courage great;
  O do with hope and patience
  Upon Jehovah wait.

TUNE: FARMER 76.76.D (30B) or
    ST. THEODULPH 76.76.D
    ("All Glory, Laud and Honor")
    (new *Trinity Hymnal*, p. 235)

Psalm 32

1 What blessedness for him
    whose guilt
  Has all forgiven been!
  When his transgressions
    pardoned are,
  And covered is his sin.
2 O blessed the man 'gainst whom
    the LORD
  Counts no iniquity,
  And in whose spirit there is not
  Deceit or treachery.

3 When I kept silent,
    my bones aged;
  My groaning filled each day.
4 Your hand oppressed me
    day and night;
  My moisture dried away.
5 Then I to You admitted sin,
  Hid not my guiltiness;
  I said, "I will before the LORD
  Transgressions now confess."

  Then You did all my sin forgive
  And take my guilt away.
6 For this when You are
    near at hand
  Let all the godly pray.
  The rising floods will harm
    him not.
7 You are my hiding place.
  And You will comfort me
    with songs
  Of victory and grace.

8 Instruction I will give to you
  And teach you as you go.
  My watchful eye will guide
    your steps;
  My counsel you will know.
9 Be not like senseless horse
    or mule
  Which if you would subdue
  You must with bit and bridle hold
  To bring him close to you.

10 The wicked many pangs endure,
  But steadfast cov'nant love
  Encircles ev'ry man whose trust
  Is in the LORD above.
11 Be glad and shout, you
    righteous ones,
  And in the LORD rejoice!
  And all whose hearts are
    just and true
  Sing out with joyful voice.

TUNE: VOX DILECTI CMD (32C)
("I Heard the Voice of Jesus Say")

Psalm 33

Verses 1–11

1 You righteous, praise the LORD
    with joy;
  It's good that just men
    praise employ.
2 With thanks the LORD O praise!
  The harp and ten–stringed viol
    bring,
3 With skill resounding praises sing;
  A new song to Him raise.

4 For upright is Jehovah's word,
  He does in all His work record
  His faithfulness and worth.
5 In justice and in doing right
  Jehovah always takes delight.
  His mercy fills the earth.

6 Jehovah's word the
    heavens made,
  And all the host of them arrayed
  His breath has caused to be.
7 He rolls the waters heap on heap;
  He gathers all the mighty deep
  In caverns of the sea.

8 Let all the earth Jehovah fear;
  Let all that dwell both
    far and near
  In awe before Him stand.
9 When He had spoken it
    was done,
  And finished was each
    work begun
  When once He gave command.

10 He made the nations'
    counsel vain;
The plots the heathen
    would maintain
Jehovah caused to fail.
11 Jehovah's counsel shall endure;
His purposes of heart most sure
Though ages all prevail.

Verses 12–22

12 O truly is the nation blessed
Whose God, before the world
    confessed,
Jehovah is alone;
And blessed the people is
    whom He
Has made His heritage to be
And chosen for His own.

13 The LORD looks forth from
    heaven high;
On sons of men He turns His eye.
14 There seated on His throne
He looks to earth on all mankind.
15 As one He fashions every mind;
To Him their deeds are known.

16 No king is saved by
    gathered hosts;
No great strength which the
    mighty boasts
His safety can provide.
17 It's vain to trust the warlike steed
Which cannot by his strength
    or speed
Achieve the rescue tried.

18 On those who worship Him in fear
And trust His lovingkindness here
The LORD has set His eye,
19 That He may save their soul
    from death
And keep them living by
    His breath
When famine bids them die.

20 Our soul is waiting for the LORD.
Our shield, He will us help afford.
21 In Him our heart's elate,
Because we trust His holy name.

22 Your mercy, LORD, O let us claim,
As we upon You wait.

TUNE: RAVENDALE 886.886. (33A)

Based on the *Book of Psalms,* 1871 and
The Psalter, 1912

Psalm 34

Verses 1–14

1 In every time I'll always bless
    the LORD;
His praise will ever be
    within my mouth.
2 My soul will make its boasting
    in the LORD;
Let all the humble hear it
    and be glad.
3 O join with me to magnify the LORD!
Let us together raise His name
    on high!

4 I sought the LORD
    and He has answered me,
And He from all my terrors
    set me free.
5 O look to Him,
    be ra-diant, unashamed!
6 This poor man cried;
    the LORD from trouble saved.
7 The LORD's own angel
    constantly encamps
Around those fearing Him,
    and rescues them.

8 O taste and you
    will see the LORD is good!
How happy is the man who
    trusts in Him!
9 O fear the LORD,
    all you He has redeemed!
For those who fear Him never
    suffer want.
10 Young lions hunger;
    they may lack their food;
But those who seek the LORD shall
    have no want.

(Continues)

11 O come, you children, listen
   unto me;
   And I will teach you how to
   fear the LORD.
12 Who longs for life
   and loves to see good days?
13 From evil keep your tongue,
   your lips from lies.
14 Depart from evil and be
   doing good;
   Seek peace and strive for it with
   all your heart.

Verses 15–22

15 Jehovah's eyes
   are toward the righteous ones;
   His ears are open to their
   ev'ry cry.
16 The LORD's face is against
   all evil men
   To cut off memory of them
   from earth.
17 The righteous cry;
   Jehovah hears and saves;
   From all their troubles He
   delivers them.

18 The LORD is near to ev'ry
   broken heart,
   And those who are in spirit
   crushed He saves.
19 Though many are the trials
   of the just,
   The LORD delivers him from
   ev'ry one.
20 For He is safely keeping all
   his bones;
   Not one of them can ever
   broken be.

21 But evil surely shall the
   wicked slay,
   And those who hate the just will
   be condemned.
22 The LORD provides
   redemption for the soul
   Of everyone who truly
   serves His will,
   And none will be
   condemned among all those

Who for their only refuge
fly to Him.

TUNE: YORKSHIRE 10.10.10.10.10.10.
(34C)

Psalm 35

Verses 1–8

1 Plead, LORD, against contending
   foes,
   And fight with them who
   fight with me.
2 Take hold of buckler and
   of shield;
   Rise up and my defender be.
3 Draw out the spear and stop
   the way
   Against the men pursuing me;
   And to my soul in mercy say,
   "I am salvation unto Thee."

4 Let those who seek to
   take my soul
   Themselves be humbled,
   shamed of face;
   Let them be thwarted and
   turned back
   Who are devising my disgrace.
5 Let them be chaff before
   the wind,
   Jehovah's angel driving them;
6 All dark and slipp'ry be their way,
   Jehovah's angel chasing them.

7 Without a cause their net they hid
   To take me in the pit prepared.
   Without a cause they dug a pit
   In which my soul might
   be ensnared.
8 Let him the unexpected meet;
   Let him be caught within
   the snare
   Which he has spread for
   other feet,
   And fall to desolation there.

Verses 9–18

9 My soul shall in the LORD rejoice,
In His salvation boastful be;
10 Exulting, all my bones will say,
"Jehovah, who is like to Thee?
For Thou the poor deliverest
From one who is for him
too strong;
The poor and needy Thou
dost spare
From one who'd rob or do
him wrong."

11 False witnesses against me stood,
Of things I knew not
charges made.
12 They gave me evil for my good;
To rob my soul they ill repaid.
13 But I, in sackcloth I was clad,
When they in sickness
suffered pain;
I made my soul with fasting sad;
My prayers return to me again.

14 As though for friend or
brother near,
In their distress I grieved aloud;
As one who mourns
a mother dear
With deepest sorrow
I was bowed.
15 But when I stumbled
they rejoiced,
And secretly they met to plot;
And injured ones their
malice voiced,
With slander tore me, ceasing not.

16 As godless jesters at a feast
They with their teeth have
gnashed at me.
17 How long, O Lord, wilt Thou
look on?
Wilt Thou unheeding all this see?
From their destruction
pluck my soul,
And snatch my life from
lions strong.

18 Then with the saints I'll
give Thee thanks.
And praise Thee in the mighty
throng.

Verses 19–28

19 Let not my wrongful enemies
Raise over me their joyful cries,
Nor those whose hate I merit not
With secret scorning wink
their eyes.
20 They speak not peace;
deceit they plot
Against the men of peaceful mien;
21 They open wide their mouth at me
And say, "Aha! Our eyes
have seen!"

22 LORD, Thou hast seen;
then be not still!
O Lord, be not far from my sight!
23 Stir up Thyself! To justice wake!
My God, my Lord,
uphold my right!
24 Judge me in justice, LORD my God,
And let them not rejoice in me,
25 Nor say in heart, "He is devour'd!
Behold, our soul's desire we see!"

26 Let them be shamed and
humbled all
Who joy at my calamity;
Let them be clothed with shame,
disgrace,
Who magnify themselves o'er me.
27 But let them shout and
loud rejoice
Who long to see me justified;
And let them say with
ceaseless voice,
"The LORD be ever magnified!

Because He loves His
servant's peace!"
28 And thus my tongue will meditate
Upon Thy perfect righteousness,
And all the day Thy praise relate.

TUNE: HAMBURG LM (35A)
("When I Survey the Wondrous Cross")

27

Psalm 36

Verses 1–6a

1 Transgression to the
    wicked speaks;
Deep in the heart it lies.
There surely is no fear of God
At all before his eyes,

2 Because himself he flatters so
In his own blinded eyes,
That he in his iniquity
Sees nothing to despise.

3 The words he utters with
    his mouth
Are wickedness and lies;
He has refrained from doing good
And ceases to be wise.

4 His thoughts and plans upon
    his bed
Iniquity invent;
He sets himself in ways not good,
From evil won't relent.

5 Thy mercy, LORD, extends
    to heav'n;
6 Thy faithfulness, the sky.
Thy justice is like mounts of God;
Thy judgments depths defy.

Verses 6b–12

LORD, Thou preservest man
    and beast.
7 How precious, God, Thy grace!
Beneath the shadow of Thy wings
Men's sons their trust shall place.

8 They with the bounty
    of Thy house
Shall be well satisfied;
From rivers full of Thy delights
Thou dost their drink provide.

9 Because the fountain filled
    with life
Is only found with Thee;

And in that purest light of Thine
We clearly light shall see.

10 To them that know Thee,
    evermore
Thy lovingkindness show,
And still on men of upright heart
Thy righteousness bestow.

11 Let not the foot of pride crush me,
Nor wicked hand detain.
12 There evildoers fall; thrust down,
They cannot rise again.

TUNE: MANOAH CM (36A)
("When All Your Mercies")

Based on *The Psalter*, 1912

Psalm 37

Verses 1–9

1 Have no disturbing thoughts about
Those doing wickedly,
And be not envious of those
Who work iniquity.
2 For even like the growing grass
Soon be cut down shall they;
And like the green and
    tender plant
They all shall fade away.

3 Set thou thy trust upon the LORD;
Continue doing good.
Dwell thou securely in the land;
Make faithfulness thy food.
4 Joy in the LORD; He'll grant
    each gift
For which thy heart may call.
5 Commit thy way unto the LORD;
Trust Him; He'll do it all.

6 And like the morning light
    He shall
Thy righteousness display;
And He thy judgment
    shall bring forth
Like noontide of the day.
7 Rest in the LORD; wait patiently;

Fret not for anyone
Who prospers in his wicked way,
Completing schemes begun.

8 Cease being thou by anger stirred;
Make thou of wrath an end.
Fret not thyself, for fretting will
To evildoing tend.

9 For evildoers soon shall be
Cut off, no more to stand;
But those who wait upon the Lord
Inherit shall the land.

Verses 10–19

10 For yet a little while, and then
The wicked shall not be;
His place thou shalt consider well,
But him thou shalt not see.

11 The meek and humble of the land
Inheritors shall be;
And they shall then delight
   themselves
In full prosperity.

12 The wicked plots against the just
And grinds his teeth in wrath;

13 Because He sees his day will come
The Lord at him shall laugh.

14 The wicked men have drawn
   their swords
And bent their bows to slay,
To cast the needy down and kill
The men of upright way.

15 But yet the sword which they
   have drawn
Shall enter their own heart;
Their bows which they are
   bending shall
In broken pieces part.

16 The little that the righteous has
Is more and better far
Than great abundance many have
Who wholly wicked are.

17 For wicked arms shall broken be;
The Lord the just sustains.

18 The Lord knows days of
   perfect men;
Their heritage remains.

19 They shall not be ashamed
   when they
The time of evil see;
And when the days of
   famine come
They satisfied shall be.

Verses 20–28

20 But wicked men, Jehovah's foes,
Like meadow flow'rs are they;
And they shall vanish;
   as does smoke
They all shall fade away.

21 The wicked borrows, but his debt
He never does repay;
Whereas the righteous gracious is
And freely gives away.

22 For those who have been
   blessed by Him
Inherit shall the land;
And those who have been
   cursed by Him,
Cut off, shall no more stand.

23 The very steps of man have been
Established by the Lord;
He takes great pleasure
   in man's way,
His progress to record.

24 Though he may stumble, he shall
   not
Fall so he cannot stand,
Because Jehovah is the One
Who holds him by his hand.

25 I have been young, now
   many years
Have o'er my life been spread;
I've never seen the righteous left,
His children begging bread.

26 All day he's gracious and he lends;
His sons a blessing are.

27 Depart from evil, and do good,
And dwell for evermore.

28 Because Jehovah justice loves
And never leaves His own,
They are preserved for evermore,
But sinners overthrown.

(Turn page for next section)

29 The righteous shall inherit earth,
   And ever in it dwell.
30 The just man's mouth will
      wisdom speak;
   His tongue will justice tell.
31 The law of God is in his heart;
   No stumbling steps he'll make.
32 The wicked spies upon the just
   And seeks his life to take.

33 The Lord will never leave the just
   Within the wicked's hands,
   Nor let the righteous be
      condemned
   When he in judgment stands.
34 Wait on the Lord and keep
      His way;
   Exalt you then shall He
   That you inherit shall the land,
   The wicked's ruin see.

35 I saw the wicked, ruthless man,
   A tree whose leaves abound;
36 I passed one day and he
      was gone;
   Though sought, could not
      be found.
37 Consider well the perfect man;
   The upright watch and see;
   For certainly the man of peace
   Shall have posterity.

38 But those who are transgressors
      will
   Be wiped out one and all.
   Posterity of wicked men
   Will be cut off and fall.
39 Salvation of the righteous ones
   Is from the Lord alone.
   He will a perfect refuge be
   In times distress is known.

40 Jehovah helps and rescues them;
   He will deliver them
   From wicked men; He will
      them save
   Because they trust in Him.

1 *Have no disturbing*
     thoughts about
  Those doing wickedly,
  And be not envious of those
  Who work iniquity.

TUNE: FOREST GREEN CMD (40C)

Elements from *Scottish Psalter*, 1650

Psalm 38

Verses 1–10

1 Lord, do not in hot displeasure
  Speak in stern reproof to me;
  Let Thy chast'ning be in measure
  And Thy stroke from anger free.
2 For Thy hand most sorely presses;
  Fast Thine arrows stick within;
3 Wrath my weary flesh distresses,
  Gives my bones no rest for sin.

4 For my manifold transgressions
  Have gone up above my head;
  Like a burden their oppressions
  Weigh me down with
      constant dread.
5 Loathsome are my wounds
      neglected;
  My own folly makes it so;
6 Bowed with pain, with grief
      dejected,
  All day long I mourning go.

7 For my loins are filled
      with burning,
  All my flesh with sore distress;
8 Faint and bruised, I'm
      ever mourning
  In my heart's disquietness.
9 My desire and ceaseless wailing,
  Lord, unveiled before Thee lie;
10 Throbs my heart; my strength
      is failing;
  All the light has left my eye.

11 Friends and lovers whom
   I cherish
   From my plague now stand aloof;
   My own kinsmen, though I perish,
   Come no more beneath my roof.
12 They that for my life are seeking
   Snares for me in secret lay,
   Hurtful things against me
      speaking,
   Plots devising all the day.

13 As one deaf and dumb appearing
   Naught I hear, nor silence break;
14 I'm as one their words
      not hearing,
   And whose lips no answer make.
15 Lord my God, in Thee I'm
      trusting;
   Thou, O Lord, wilt answer me;
16 Lest they joy, against me boasting,
   When my slipping feet they see.

17 Since I ready am to stumble,
   Ever with me grief has been;
18 Guilt I'll own with spirit humble,
   And be sorry for my sin.
19 Full of life and great in number,
   Strong the foes who me
      withstood;
20 Evil they for kindness render,
   Hating me for doing good.

21 O my God, do not forsake me;
   O Jehovah, be Thou near;
22 To my helper I betake me;
   As my Savior, Lord, appear.

TUNE: CHARLESTOWN 87.87. (119G)
      or MERTON 87.87.
   (*Psalter Hymnal* [4th ed.], p. 332)

Based on the *Book of Psalms,* 1871

Psalm 39

1 "I will take heed and guard
   my ways," I said,
   "So that my tongue no sinful
   word shall stain;
   As with a bridle I will keep
   my mouth,
   While in my presence wicked
   men remain."

2 In silence dumb I ceased from
   speaking good;
   My heart within was hot,
   my sorrow stirred;
3 And while I mused the fire
   began to burn;
   Then spake I with my tongue
   this earnest word:

4 "My end, O Lord, and measure
   of my days
   Make me to know, and thus my
   frailty see.
5 Lo, Thou hast made my days an
   handbreadth long;
   My lifetime is a nothing
   unto Thee.

6 "Each man at best is
   altogether vain.
   Each man doth surely walk
   in empty show;
   They heap up wealth and vex
   themselves for naught,
   Nor know to whom their
   garnered riches go.

(Turn page for next section)

7   "And now, O Lord, what wait
      I longer for?
    My expectation ever is in Thee;
8   Deliver me from all my sinfulness;
    The scorn of foolish men O make
      not me.

9   "Yes, I was dumb; I opened
      not my mouth,
    Because this work was done
      at Thy command.
10 But now remove Thy stroke away
      from me;
    I am consumed beneath Thy
      smiting hand.

11 "Thou with rebukes dost chasten
      man for sin;
    His beauty fades beneath the
      touch of death;
    It is consumed as by the fretting
      moth.
    Oh, surely every man is
      but a breath.

12 "Lord, hear my prayers; heed
      Thou my cry and tears;
    A stranger here I pass as
      all before.
13 O spare me that I may
      recover strength
    Before I go away and be
      no more."

TUNE: EVENTIDE 10.10.10.10. (39B)
("Abide with Me")

Psalm 40

Verses 1–9

1   I waited for the Lord;
    He stooped and heard my cry.
2   He brought me from the pit,
    Out of the dungeon mire,
    My feet set on a rock,
    My footsteps made secure.
3   My lips He gave a song,
    A song to praise our God.

    Many will see with awe,
    And so will trust the Lord.
4   Blessed he who trusts in God,
    And turns not to false men.
5   You have worked wonders, Lord;
    No one compares to You!
    Should I declare each one,
    Their number is too great.

6   You want no offering,
    Nor ask a sacrifice,
    But You have given me
    A ready ear to hear
    You ask no off'rings burnt
    Nor sacrifice for sin.
7   So I say, "Here I come,
    As in the scroll inscribed.

8   "To do Your will, O God,
    To me is my delight.
    Your law is part of me,
    Deep in my heart, O God."
9   In congregation great
    I told Your righteousness.
    You know, Lord, I spoke out;
    I did not close my lips.

Verses 10–17

10 I hid not in my heart
    Your truth and saving help;
    Your faithfulness I preached
    In the assembly great.
11 You'll not withhold from me
    Your tender mercies, Lord,
    And Your unfailing love
    Will ever keep me safe.

12 Misfortunes beyond count
Have taken hold of me.
My sins close in on me
So that I cannot see.
In greater sum are they
Than hairs upon my head.
So my heart fails in me;
My courage fades away.

13 Come to my rescue, LORD;
O LORD, make haste to help.
14 Let all who seek my life
Be shamed and be confused.
Let them fall back in shame
Who want to see my hurt;
15 Let them be dumb who jeer,
"Aha, Aha" to me.

16 Let all men who seek You
Be glad and in You joy;
Who Your salvation love
Say, "Glory to the LORD!"
17 Though I'm in want and poor,
The Lord takes thought of me.
My Help, my Savior, come!
O God, do not delay!

TUNE: I NEED THEE 66.66.D (143B)
("I Need Thee Every Hour")

Psalm 41

Verses 1–6

1 How blessed the man who
guides the poor
By counsel strong and clear;
The LORD will surely rescue him
When evil days draw near.
2 The LORD will guard him in
the land;
His life is blessed indeed;
Nor will You let him fall before
His adversaries' greed.

3 The LORD sustains him on his bed
Of sickness and of pain.
And from his bed You make
him rise;

He will his health regain.
4 Now as for me, I said, "O LORD,
Have mercy on my soul.
Because against You have
I sinned,
Restore and make me whole."

5 My foes speak evil things of me
And to each other say,
"When will he die; when will
his name
Completely pass away?"
6 And when he comes to see
me here
His words are all deceit.
He gathers evil in his heart
And tells it in the street.

Verses 7–13

7 All those who hate me whisper ill,
Against me harm devise.
8 "Some evil holds him fast,"
they say,
"Brought down he will not rise."
9 And even my familiar friend
In whom my trust was real,
The one who ate my bread,
has turned
And lifted up his heel.

10 But You, O LORD, be merciful
And raise me in Your grace;
And then a recompense complete
Upon them I will place.
11 By this I know that I am held
As precious in Your eyes;
My foes do not raise over me
Their glad exulting cries.

12 And thus am I sustained by You
To be complete and well,
And in Your presence evermore
You make me safely dwell.
13 The LORD, the God of Is-ra-el,
Be blessed and blessed again
From age to everlasting age.
Amen, and still Amen.

TUNE: SALZBURG CM (115A)

Psalm 42

Verses 1–5

1 As in its thirst a fainting hart
   To water brooks doth flee,
   So pants my longing soul, O God,
   That I may come to Thee.
2 My soul for God, the living God,
   Is thirsting; shall I near
   Before the face of God approach
   And in His sight appear?

3 My tears have unto me been food
   Both in the night and day,
   While unto me continu'lly,
   "Where is your God?" they say.
4 Poured out within me is my soul
   When this I think upon:
   How often with the eager throng
   I rev'rently had gone,

   How to the house of God I went
   With voice of joy and praise,
   Yea, with the multitude that kept
   The solemn holy days.
5 O why, my soul, art thou
      bowed down?
   Why so discouraged be?
   Hope now in God!
      I'll praise Him still!
   My help, my God is He!

Verses 6–11

6 O God, my soul's cast down
      in me;
   I Thee remember will
   From Jordan land, from Hermon's
      height,
   And ev'n from Mizar hill.
7 With thunder of Thy waterfalls
   Deep unto deep doth call;
   Thy billows all roll over me;
   On me Thy breakers fall.

8 And yet Jehovah will command
   His mercy in the day;
   By night His song shall be
      with me;
   To God, my Life, I'll pray.

9 To God Who is my rock I'll say,
   "O why forget me so?
   Beneath oppression of my foes
   Why do I mourning go?"

10 As with a sword within my bones
   My enemies upbraid,
   While unto me, "Where is
      Thy God?"
   Continu'lly is said.
11 O why, my soul, art thou
      bowed down?
   Why so discouraged be?
   Hope now in God!
      I'll praise Him still!
   My Help, my God is He!

TUNE: ST. AGNES CM (42A)
("Jesus the Very Thought of Thee")

Based on *Scottish Psalter*, 1650

34

Psalm 43

1 Defend me, God, and plead
   my case
Against a godless clan;
Deliver me from fraudulent,
Unjust and wicked man.

2 O God in Whom I refuge take,
Why have You cast me off?
Why must I grieving walk about
While foes oppress and scoff?

3 O send Your light forth and
   Your truth;
O let them lead me well
And bring me to Your holy hill,
The place You choose to dwell.

4 Then I will to God's altar go,
To God, my boundless joy.
To render thanks to God,
   my God,
The harp I will employ.

5 O why, my soul, are you
   bowed down?
Why so discouraged be?
Hope now in God! I'll praise
   Him still!
My Help, my God is He!

TUNE: ST. AGNES CM (42A)
("Jesus the Very Thought of Thee")

Based on *Scottish Psalter*, 1650

Psalm 44

Verses 1–8

1 O God, we have heard and our
   fathers have told
What wonders You did in the
   great days of old.
2 Where nations were crushed and
   cast out by Your hand;
You planted our fathers to dwell
   in the land.

3 They gained not the land by the
   edge of their sword;
Their own arm to them could no
   safety afford,
But Your right hand, Your arm,
   the light of Your face.
You showed them Your favor,
   Your wonderful grace.

4 O God, You alone are forever
   my King;
Command, and for Jacob
   deliverance bring.
5 Through You we will surely
   put down all our foes,
Through Your name will trample
   on them that oppose.

6 No trust will I place in my sword
   or my bow,
7 For You are our Savior from hater
   and foe.
8 In God we will boast Who has put
   them to shame,
All day and forever give thanks to
   Your name.

(Turn page for next section)

9 But You have forsaken, to shame
brought our boasts;
No more into battle You go with
our hosts.
10 You make us turn back from the
foe in dismay,
And spoilers who hate us have
made us their prey.

11 You give us like sheep to be
slaughtered for food,
Among all the nations dispersed
and pursued.
12 You sell off Your people to
strangers for naught;
Their price to Your treas'ry no
increase has brought.

13 You make all our neighbors
reproach us in pride,
And cause those around us to
scoff and deride.
14 Our name among nations
a byword You've made;
The people all laugh at us,
shaking the head.

15 And all the day long I behold my
disgrace,
And covered am I with the shame
of my face,
16 Because the blasphemer and
scoffer I hear,
While foe and avenger against
me appear.

17 We suffered this, yet we did not
forget You;
We always have been to Your
covenant true.
18 Our heart is not turned and our
steps have not strayed,
19 Though crushed amid ruins and
under death's shade.

20 If we have forgotten the name of
our God,
Or unto an idol our hands
spread abroad,
21 Shall God not search out and
uncover this sin,
Who knows ev'ry heart and the
secrets within?

22 But all the day long for Your sake
we're consumed;
Like sheep for the slaughter to
death we are doomed.
23 Arouse Yourself! Why are You
sleeping, O LORD?
Awake? Do not leave us
forever ignored.

24 O why are You hiding the light
of Your face,
Forgetting the burden and grief
of our race?
25 Our soul is bowed down; we lie
crushed in the dust.
26 Rise! Help and redeem us! Your
mercy we trust.

TUNE: DOMINUS REGIT ME
11.11.11.11. (23D)

Based on the *Book of Psalms*, 1871 and
The Psalter, 1912

Psalm 45

Verses 1–7, 17

1 My heart doth overflow;
A noble theme I sing.
My tongue's a skillful writer's pen
To speak about the King.
2 More fair than sons of men
Thy lips with grace o'erflow,
Because His blessing evermore
Did God on Thee bestow.

3 Thy sword gird on Thy thigh,
O Thou supreme in might,
And gird Thyself with majesty
And with Thy splendor bright.
4 To victory ride forth
For meekness, truth, and right;
And may Thy right hand teach
 to Thee
The deeds of dreadful might.

5 Thine arrows sharpened are,
Men under Thee to bring,
To pierce the heart of enemies
Who fight against the King.
6 Thy royal throne, O God,
From everlasting is;
A righteous scepter evermore
Thy kingdom's scepter is.

7 Thou righteousness hast loved
And wickedness abhorred;
On Thee, 'bove all, has God,
 Thy God,
The oil of gladness poured.
17 Through every coming age
I'll make Thy name to live;
The peoples therefore evermore
Their praise to Thee shall give.

Verses 8–17

8 With ca-sia, aloes, myrrh,
Thy robes sweet fragrance had;
From palaces of i-vo-ry
The sweet harps made Thee glad.
9 King's daughters are among
Those who in honor stand.

Thy bride arrayed in Ophir gold
There stands at Thy right hand.

10 O daughter, hear and heed;
Incline to me thine ear:
"Forget thou now thy people all,
Thy father's household dear.
11 Thy beauty to the King
Shall then delightful be;
Because He is thy Lord, do thou
To Him bow rev'rently."

12 The daughter then of Tyre
There with a gift shall be,
And all the wealthy of the land
Will make requests of Thee.
13 The daughter of the King
All glorious waits within;
Her lovely gown with threads
 of gold
Has interwoven been.

14 She to the King is led
In fine embroidery;
The bridesmaids in her train,
 her friends,
Are brought to honor Thee.
15 Attendants following
Their joy and gladness bring,
Until they all have entered there
The palace of the King.

16 Then in Thy fathers' stead
Thy children Thou shalt take
And everywhere in all the earth
Them noble princes make.
17 Through every coming age
I'll make Thy name to live;
The peoples therefore evermore
Their praise to Thee shall give.

TUNE: DIADEMATA SMD (45C)
("Crown Him with Many Crowns")

Elements from *Scottish Psalter*, 1650 and
The Psalter, 1912

37

Psalm 46

First Version

1　God is our refuge and our strength,
　　In straits a present aid;
2　And, therefore, tho' the
　　　　earth remove
　　We will not be afraid;
　　Tho' hills amidst the seas be cast,
3　Tho' troubled waters roar,
　　Yea, tho' the swelling
　　　　billows shake
　　The mountains on the shore.

4　A river is whose streams make glad
　　The city of our God,
　　The holy place wherein the Lord
　　Most High has His abode.
5　Yea, God is in the midst of her;
　　Unmoved she stands for aye;
　　And God will surely grant her help
　　Before the break of day.

6　The nations raged; the
　　　　kingdoms moved;
　　And when the earth had heard
　　The mighty voice He sent abroad
　　It melted at His word.
7　The Lord of hosts is on our side
　　Our safety to secure;
　　The God of Jacob is for us
　　A refuge strong and sure.

8　O come, behold what
　　　　wondrous works
　　Have by the Lord been wrought;
　　Come, see what desolations great
　　He on the earth has brought.
9　To utmost ends of all the earth
　　Wars into peace He turns;
　　The bow He breaks, the spear
　　　　He cuts,
　　In fire the char-iot burns.

10　Be still and know that I am God;
　　Among the nations I
　　Will be exalted; I on earth
　　Will be exalted high.
11　The Lord of hosts is on our side.

Our safety to secure;
The God of Jacob is for us
A refuge strong and sure.

TUNE: MATERNA CMD (46A)
("O Beautiful for Spacious Skies")

Based on *Scottish Psalter*, 1650

Psalm 46

Second Version

1　God is our refuge and our strength,
　　A present help in our distress.
2　We will not therefore be afraid
　　Tho' all the earth should
　　　　be removed,
　　Tho' mountains great be hurled
　　Into the ocean's depths,
3　Tho' seas may roar and foam
　　And billows shake the shore,
　　Tho' mountains tremble at
　　　　their power.

4　A river brings refreshing streams
　　To cheer the city of our God,
　　The Most High's holy
　　　　dwelling place.
5　God is in her; she won't be moved;
　　At dawn will God help her.
6　The heathen rage; realms quake;
　　He lifts his voice; earth melts.
7　The Lord of hosts with us!
　　Our fortress strong is Jacob's God.

8　O come, see what the Lord
　　　　has done:
　　He desolations brought on earth;
9　On earth He puts an end to wars,
　　Breaks bow and spear, and
　　　　char-iots burns.
10　Be still! Know I am God.
　　Exalted o'er all men,
　　Exalted o'er all earth.
11　The Lord of hosts with us!
　　Our fortress strong is Jacob's God.

TUNE: EIN' FESTE BURG 88.88.66.668. (46C)
("A Mighty Fortress Is Our God")

Psalm 47

1 All peoples, clap your hands
    for joy;
  To God in triumph shout;
2 For awesome is the
    LORD Most High,
  Great King the earth throughout.
3 He brings the peoples under us
  In mastery complete;
  And He it is Who nations all
  Subdues beneath our feet.

4 The land of our inheritance
  He chooses out for us,
  And He to us the glory gives
  Of Jacob whom He loves.
5 God is ascended with a shout,
  The LORD with trumpeting.
6 Sing praises unto God! Sing praise!
  Sing praises to our King!

7 For God is King of all the earth;
  Sing praise with skillfulness.
8 God rules the nations; God sits on
  His throne of holiness.
9 Assemble, men of Abrah'm's God!
  Come, people, princes, nigh!
  The shields of earth belong to God;
  He is exalted high.

TUNE: PETERSHAM CMD (47A)

Based on *Scottish Psalter,* 1650

Psalm 48

Verses 1–8

1 The LORD is great! Much to
    be praised
  In our God's city, and
    where stands
2 Most fair upon His holy hill
  Mount Zion, joy of all the earth!

  She is the place where
    God resides,
  The city of the Mighty King.
3 God in her fortresses is known
  To be a refuge safe and sure.

4 For, lo, the kings their
    forces joined,
  Advancing, marched, with
    confidence,
5 But, seeing her, they were amazed;
  In terror they were put to flight.

6 There trembling seized its hold
    on them,
  Pangs like a woman giving birth.
7 For You with wind out of the east
  The mighty Tarshish ships destroy.

8 As we have heard, so we
    have seen
  Within the Mighty LORD's abode,
  Within the city of our God:
  God keeps her safe for evermore.

Verses 9–14

9 O God, Your cov'nant love to us
  We've thought on in Your
    temple's courts.
10 O God, Your praise, just like
    Your name,
  Extends to earth's remotest bounds.

11 Your right hand's full
    of righteousness.
  O let Mount Zion now rejoice;
  Let Judah's villages be glad,
  For all Your judgments are
    most just.

12 Encircle Zion, walk about;
  Her towers count, her ramparts
    note;
13 Go through her fortresses with care,
  And to your sons their story tell.

  The one true God, He is our God,
14 And evermore He is the same;
  He surely will us safely keep
  And He will guide us on
    through death.

TUNE: WAREHAM LM (35B)
("Great God We Sing")

The Complete Book of Psalms for Singing,
1991; altered 1994

Psalm 49

Verses 1–9

1 Hear this, all ye peoples, hear;
Earth's inhabitants, give ear;
2 All of high and low degree,
Rich and poor, give ear to me.

3 For my mouth shall
wisdom speak:
Knowledge with my heart
I'll seek,
4 Lend to parables my ear,
With the harp make dark
things clear.

5 Why should I to fear give way
When I see the evil day,
When with wickedness my foes
Shall surround me and oppose?

6 They that trust in treasured gold,
Though they boast of
wealth untold,
7 None can bid his brother live,
None to God a ransom give;

8 Life's redemption—high its price!
Nothing can for it suffice,
9 That from death one should
be free
And corruption never see.

Verses 10–20

10 For alike before their eyes
Die the foolish and the wise;
Then their riches' hoarded heap,
Other hands in turn shall keep.

11 Yet within their heart they say
That their houses are for aye,
That their dwelling places grand
Shall for generations stand.

To their lands they give
their name,
In the hope of lasting fame;
12 But man's honor quickly flies.
He, like beasts that perish, dies.

13 Though this folly marks
their ways,
Though the world their
sayings praise,
14 In the grave like sheep
they're laid;
Death their shepherd there
is made.

O'er them soon shall rule the just,
All their beauty turn to dust;
15 But from death God will retrieve,
To Himself my soul receive.

16 Let no fear disturb your peace;
Though one's house and
wealth increase,
17 Death shall all his glory end;
Naught shall after him descend.

18 Though the world his praise
will tell,
When to self he doeth well,
And though while of life
possessed,
He his soul has always blessed,

19 With his fathers he shall lie,
Where no light shall meet his eye.
20 Man in honor when not wise,
Like the beasts that perish, dies.

TUNE: MERCY 77.77. (49B)
("Cast Your Burdens on the Lord")

Based on the *Book of Psalms*, 1871 and
The Psalter, 1912

Psalm 50

Verses 1–6

1 The mighty God the Lord
  Has spoken and did call
  The earth from rising of the sun
  To where it has its fall.
2 From Zion's holy hill,
  Perfection's high abode
  Of matchless beauty, even thence
  In glory shineth God.

3 Our God shall surely come;
  Keep silence shall not He;
  Before Him fire shall waste;
     great storms
  Shall round about Him be.
4 And to the heav'ns above
  He sendeth forth His call,
  And also to the earth, that He
  May judge His people all.

5 "Together let My saints
  Before Me gathered be;
  Those that by sacrifice have made
  A covenant with Me."
6 Then shall the heav'ns declare
  His righteousness abroad,
  Because He only is the judge;
  Yea, none is judge but God.

7 "O ye, My people, hear;
  I'll speak and testify
  Against thee, O thou Is-ra-el,
  For God, thy God, am I.
8 "For sacrifices I
  No blame will on thee lay,
  Nor for burnt offerings of thine
  Before Me every day.

9 "I'll take no calf nor goat
  From house or fold of thine;
10 For cattle on a thousand hills
  And all wild beasts are Mine.
11 "The birds of mountains great
  Are all to Me well known;
  The beasts that roam the
     field untamed,
  They, too, are all My own.

12 "Then if I hungry were
  I would not tell it thee,
  Because the world with
     all its wealth
  Belongeth unto Me.
13 "Will I eat flesh of bulls?
  Or goats' blood drink will I?
14 Thanksgiving offer thou, and pay
  Thy vows to God Most High.

15 "And do thou call on Me
  When troublous days draw nigh;
  To thee I'll give deliverance;
  Thou shalt Me glorify."

(Turn page for next section)

16　But to the wicked man
　　Saith God, "How dost thou dare
　　To take My cov'nant in
　　　　Thy mouth,
　　My statutes to declare
17　Since thou dost even hate
　　The warnings thou hast heard,
　　And thou hast thrown behind
　　　　thy back
　　The teachings of My word?

18　"Thou gavest thy consent
　　When thou a thief hast seen;
　　And with the vile adulterer
　　Thou hast partaker been.
19　Thy mouth to ill is giv'n;
　　Thy tongue deceit doth frame,
20　Thou dost against thy
　　　　brother speak,
　　Thy mother's son defame.

21　"Because I silence kept
　　While thou these things
　　　　hast wrought,
　　That I was wholly like thyself
　　Has been thy very thought.
　　"Yet I will thee reprove
　　And set before thine eyes,
　　Arrayed in order, thy misdeeds
　　And thine iniquities.

22　"Now ye that God forget,
　　Consider this with care,
　　Lest I when there is none to save
　　Should you in pieces tear.
23　He honors Me who brings
　　The sacrifice of praise,
　　I'll God's salvation show to him
　　Who orders right his ways."

　　TUNE: ST. THOMAS SM (50B)
　　("I Love Thy Kingdom Lord")

　Based on the *Book of Psalms,* 1871 and
　　　　Irish Psalter, 1880

1　God, be merciful to me;
　　On Thy grace I rest my plea;
　　In Thy vast, abounding grace,
　　My transgressions all erase.
2　Wash me wholly from my sin;
　　Cleanse from every ill within.

3　For my sins before me rise,
　　Ever present to my eyes.
4　I have sinned 'gainst Thee alone,
　　In Thy sight this evil done;
　　That Thy judgment may be clear,
　　And Thy sentence just appear.

5　Lo, brought forth was I in sin;
　　When conceived I was unclean.
6　Lo, Thou dost desire to find
　　Truth sincere within the mind:
　　And Thou wilt within my heart
　　Wisdom unto me impart.

7　Then with hyssop sprinkle me,
　　And from sin I clean shall be.
　　Wash me from its stain, and lo,
　　I shall whiter be than snow.
8　Make me hear joy's
　　　　cheering voice;
　　Make my broken bones rejoice.

9　From my sins hide Thou Thy face;
　　My iniquities erase.
10　O my God, renew my heart,
　　And a spirit right impart.
11　Cast me not away from Thee,
　　Nor Thy Spirit take from me.

12　Give salvation's joy again,
　　And a willing mind sustain.
13　Then thy perfect ways I'll show
　　That transgressors may
　　　　them know;
　　They converted then shall be;
　　Sinners shall be turned to Thee.

14 Free me from the guilt of blood,
   God, of my salvation God;
   Then with joy my tongue
      shall raise
   Songs Thy righteousness to praise.
15 Open Thou my lips, O Lord;
   Then my mouth shall praise
      accord.

16 Sacrifice Thou wilt not take,
   Else would I the off'ring make.
   Off'rings burnt bring no delight,
   But a broken heart, contrite,
17 God's accepted sacrifice,
   Thou, O God, wilt not despise.

18 Prosper Zion in Thy grace;
   Salem's broken walls replace.
19 Then shall sacrifices right,
   Whole burnt off'rings Thee
      delight;
   So will men, their vows to pay,
   Bullocks on Thine altar lay.

TUNE: REDHEAD/
AJALON 77.77.77. (51E)
("Gracious Spirit, Dwell With Me")

Based on the *Book of Psalms*, 1871 and
The Psalter, 1912

Psalm 52

1 Why boast yourself,
    O mighty man,
   Of evil and of wrong?
   The lovingkindness of our God
   Is present all day long.
2 You with your subtle tongue
      have planned
   Destruction to complete.
   Your tongue a sharpened razor is,
   A worker of deceit.

3 You cherish evil more than good
   And falsehood more than right.
4 You cherish all devouring words,
   O tongue which lies delight.
5 Forever God will pull you down,
   Will seize you with His hand,
   Will tear you from your
      dwelling place,
   Uproot you from the land.

6 The righteous will behold
    and fear,
   Will laugh at him and say,
7 "Behold the man who would
    not make
   Our God his strength and stay.
   This is the man who placed
      his trust
   In wealth's abundant store,
   And in the evil he desired
   Confirmed himself the more."

8 But I within the house of God
   Am like an olive tree,
   And in the steadfast love of God
   My trust shall ever be.
9 Forever I will give Thee thanks,
   What Thou hast done proclaim;
   In presence of Thy godly ones
   I'll wait on Thy good name.

TUNE: GRAEFENBERG CM (119L)
or LOUISE (27C)

Psalm 53

1 "There is no God," has said
   The foolish in his heart;
   Corrupt are they; their works
      are vile;
   They all from good depart.
2 Upon the sons of men
   God looked from heav'n abroad,
   To see if any understood,
   If any sought for God.

3 Together all are vile;
   They all are backward gone;
   And there is none that
      doeth good,
   No, not so much as one.
4 Have men that evil work
   No knowledge gained at all,
   Who eat my people as
      their bread,
   And on God do not call?

5 Great terror on them came,
   And they were much dismayed,
   Although there was no cause
      why they
   Should be at all afraid.
   His bones who thee besieged
   God has dispersed abroad;
   Thou hast them put to shame,
      because
   They were despised of God.

6 Let Is-r'el's help arise
   From Zion! God will bring
   His captives! Jacob shall rejoice,
   And Is-ra-el shall sing.

TUNE: BOYLSTON SM (53)
("A Charge Have I to Keep")

Based on the *Book of Psalms*, 1871

Psalm 54

1 By Your name, O God,
      now save me;
   Grant me justice by Your strength.
2 To these words of mine
      give answer;
   O my God, now hear my prayer.
3 Strangers have come up
      against me,
   Even men of violence.
   And they seek my life's
      destruction;
   God is not within their thoughts.

4 See how God has been
      my helper,
   How my Lord sustains my soul:
5 To my foes He pays back evil
   In Your truth destroy them all!
6 I will sacrifice with gladness;
   I will praise Your name, O Lord.
7 He has saved me from all trouble;
   I have looked on all my foes.

TUNE: EBENEZER 87.87.D (54B)
("O the Deep, Deep Love of Jesus")

Psalm 55

Verses 1–14

1 Give ear to this my prayer, O God,
Nor hide Thee from my cry.
2 Give answer, for I cannot rest
But must complain and sigh,
3 Because I hear the voice of foes,
Because the wicked press;
For they in anger bear a grudge
And on me bring distress.

4 Deep anguish is within my heart;
Death's terrors o'er me roll.
5 Great trembling, fearfulness,
and dread
Have overwhelmed my soul.
6 I cried, "O that I, like a dove,
Had wings to fly away.
Then would I flee and try to find
A restful place to stay.

7 "Lo, I would wander far and lodge
In some lone desert waste;
8 From stormy wind and
tempest high
I would escape in haste."
9 O swallow up their tongues,
O Lord;
Confuse them and divide;
For in the city I've seen strife
And violence abide.

10 For day and night upon her walls
The city they surround,
While mischief and iniquity
Inside of her is found.
11 A realm of vast destruction thrives
Within her very heart,
And from her streets oppression,
fraud,
And graft do not depart.

12 It was no foe reproaching me,
For that I could endure;
It was no hater rising up,
Or I could hide secure;
13 But it was thou, a man, a friend,
My colleague all along;
14 We shared sweet fellowship
and walked
To God's house in the throng.

15 Let death o'ertake them; to the pit
Alive let them depart;
For wickedness is in their house
And lives within their heart.
16 I'll call on God; the Lord will save;
17 I will complain and sigh
At ev'ning, morning, and at noon,
And He will hear my cry.

18 He will redeem my soul in love
That I in peace may be
From all the war against
me waged,
For many strive with me.
19 Yes, God will hear and
answer them;
He sits enthroned of old;
For them there is no change
of heart;
No fear of God they hold.

20 He raised his hands against
the ones
Who were at peace with him.
The covenant which he had sworn
He broke at his own whim.
21 Though smooth as butter was
his speech,
Within his heart was war;
Though soft as oil the words
he spoke,
A naked sword they bore.

22 Cast thou thy burden on the Lord,
And He shall thee sustain;
Yes, he makes sure that
still unmoved
The righteous shall remain.
23 But Thou, O God, wilt bring
them down
The pit of woe to see.
False killers live not half
their days.
But I will trust in Thee.

TUNE: ST. MATTHEW CMD (55B)
("How Vast the Benefits Divine")

Psalm 56

1 Be gracious unto me, O God;
The man of earth would
me devour.
He fights against me all day long,
Oppressing me with all his power.

2 My foes are watching day and night;
They many fight from places high.
3 The day I fear I'll trust in You.
4 The word of God I'll magnify.

In God I trust; I will not fear,
For what can mere flesh do to me?
5 All day they twist my words;
their thoughts
Are all of schemes to injure me.

6 They meet, they lurk, they mark
my steps;
They're waiting for my soul to fall.
7 For their iniquity, O God,
In wrath bring down the
nations all.

8 You count my wanderings;
my tears
You keep in precious mem-o-ry.
9 My foes shall, when I call,
turn back;
Long I have known God is for me.

10 In God, Whose word I'll
always praise.
The LORD, Whose word my praise
shall be
11 In God I trust; I will not fear,
For what can mere man do to me?

12 I'll pay my vows with thanks
to You;
From death, O God, You set
me free,
13 Kept me from falling, that with God
My walk in light of life may be.

TUNE: WINCHESTER NEW LM
(new *Trinity Hymnal*, p. 58)
("O Splendor of God's Glory")

Altered 1994

Psalm 57

Verses 1–4

1 Thy mercy, God, to me extend;
On Thy protection I depend,
And to Thy wings for shelter haste
Until this storm be overpast.
2 To Him I will in trouble cry,
The sovereign Judge and God
most high,
Who wonders hath for me begun,
And will not leave His work
undone.

3 For He from heav'n shall quell
the power
Of him who would my
life devour;
Forth shall His truth and
mercy send,
And my distracted soul defend.
4 For I with cru-el men converse,
Like hungry lions wild and fierce;
With men whose teeth are spears,
their words
Envenomed darts and two-edg'd
swords.

Verses 5–11

5 Be Thou, O God, exalted high;
And, as Thy glory fills the sky,
So be it o'er the earth displayed,
And Thou, as there, be here
obeyed!
6 To take me they their
net prepared;
My sinking soul almost despaired;
But they are fall'n, by Thy decree,
Into the pit they dug for me.

7 O God, my heart is fixed,
'tis bent,
Its thankful tribute to present;
And with my heart my voice
I'll raise
To Thee, my God, in songs
of praise.
8 Awake my glory; harp and lute,
No longer let your strings be mute;

And I, my tuneful part to take,
Will with the early dawn awake.

9 Thy praises, Lord, I will resound
   To all the listening nations round;
10 Thy mercy highest heav'n
      transcends,
   Thy truth beyond the
      clouds extends.
11 Be Thou, O God, exalted high!
   And, as Thy glory fills the sky,
   So be it o'er the earth displayed,
   And Thou, as there,
      be here obeyed.

TUNE: GERMANY (GARDINER) LM
(91D)
("Jesus, Thy Blood and Righteousness")

Irish Psalter, 1880

Psalm 58

1 You may be gods, but can
      you claim
   That you speak righteousness?
   And do you judge the sons
      of men
   In truth and uprightness?
2 No, even in your very heart
   You wickedness produce;
   On earth you weigh out with
      your hands
   Your violent abuse.

3 The wicked from their day
      of birth
   Are strangers to the way;
   They from the womb come
      speaking lies;
   They wander far astray.
4 They have the venom of a snake;
   They have an adder's ear
5 Which they have closed to
      charmers' songs;
   Skilled charmers they'll not hear.

6 O God, inside their
      opened mouths

Break off their cruel teeth;
The fangs of these young lions,
   LORD,
Tear out by roots beneath.
7 Let them like runoff waters be
   That leave the ground soon dry.
   Let arrows that he aims become
   Like headless shafts that fly.

8 Let them be like the snails
      that melt
   Along the course they run;
   Or like one prematurely born
   Who never sees the sun.
9 They are like blazing thorns
      which you
   Beneath your kettles lay,
   Whose heat is scarcely felt before
   A wind sweeps them away.

10 The just rejoices when he sees
   That vengeance is complete,
   For in the blood of wicked men
   He then will wash his feet.
11 They'll say, "There surely
      is reward
   For righteous ones of worth;
   There surely is a living God
   Who judges in the earth."

TUNE: ST. MICHEL'S CMD (58A)
("I've Found the Pearl of Greatest Price")

Psalm 59

Verses 1–9

1 Save me, my God! Protect
from foes
Now rising like a flood.
2 Deliver me from evil men;
Save me from men of blood.
3 Behold, they for my life lay wait;
Fierce men against me run;
But not for my transgression, LORD,
Nor sin that I have done.

4 Though I am guiltless, still
they run
And preparation make.
Arouse Thyself to help and see!
5 LORD God of hosts, awake!
Arise to punish nations all,
Thou God of Is-ra-el.
No mercy show to any who
Deceitfully rebel.

6 At night they come; they snarl
like dogs
That round the city stray.
7 Their mouths stretch wide; their
lips are swords:
"For who will hear?" they say.
8 But Thou, O LORD, dost laugh
at them;
Thou dost all nations mock.
9 O Thou my Strength, I'll hold
to Thee;
God is my fortress–rock.

Verses 10–17

10 In all His lovingkindness great
My God will meet with me.
God will permit me on my foes
To look triumphantly.
11 But lest my people should forget,
Do not the wicked slay,
But bring them down, O Lord,
our Shield,
And scatter them away.

12 Because of sin within their
mouths,
And words their lips let fly,
Let them be caught in their
own pride,
Because they curse and lie.
13 Destroy them in Thy wrath;
destroy,
That they may be no more.
Make known that God in
Jacob rules,
To earth's most distant shore.

14 At night they come; they snarl
like dogs
That round the city stray.
15 They search for food but are
not filled,
And, hungry, there they stay.
16 But of Thy strength I'll sing aloud,
At morn Thy mercy praise;
For Thou hast been my
refuge high,
My fort in evil days.

17 O Thou Who art my strength,
I will
Sing praises unto Thee;
For God is my defense, the God
Of grace He is to me.

TUNE: CREDITON CM (59B)

Psalm 60

Verses 1–5

1 O God, Thou hast rejected us,
Hast broken us once more.
As Thou with us hast angry been,
O once again restore.

2 For Thou hast made the earth to
quake,
Hast torn it fearfully.
O heal its gaping cracks, for, lo,
It shakes in agony!

3 For Thou hast made the people see
The hardness of distress,
And Thou hast made them drink
the wine
Of reeling drunkenness.

4 But those that fear Thee Thou
      didst give
  A banner in their sight,
  That they might rally and be firm,
  Made strong by truth and right.

5 O grant that Thy be-lov-ed ones
  May safe delivered be.
  O save them with Thy strong
      right hand,
  And do Thou answer me.

Verses 6–11

6 God in His holiness declared
  Let me exulting shout:
  "The land of Shechem I'll divide,
  And Succoth measure out.

7 "For all of Gilead is Mine;
  Manasseh, too, I own;
  My head's defense is Ephraim;
  I Judah made My throne.

8 "My washbowl I will Moab make,
  On Edom throw My shoe;
  O Palestine, because of Me
  Let shouts break forth from you!"

9 O who will bring me in the town
  Beseiged and fortified?
  And who as far as Edom's walls
  Will there my footsteps guide?

10 But hast Thou not indeed, O God,
  Rejected us once more?
  And wilt Thou not again, O God,
  Go forth with us to war?

11 Give help against the enemy,
  For man no help bestows.
  Through God we shall
      do valiantly,
  For He treads down our foes.

TUNE: BANGOR CM
(Psalter Hymnal [4th ed.], p. 298) or
DOWNS CM (60A)
("Happy the Home When God is There")

Elements from *The Psalter,* 1912

Psalm 61

1 My voice and prayer, O God,
      attend;
2 From ends of earth to Thee I send
  My supplicating cry,
  When troubles overwhelm
      my breast;
  Then lead me on the rock to rest
  That higher is than I.

3 In Thee my soul has
      shelter found,
  And Thou hast been from
      foes around
  The tower to which I flee.
4 Within Thy house I will abide,
  And underneath Thy wings
      will hide,
  Forever safe in Thee.

5 For Thou, O God, my vows
      hast heard,
  On me the heritage conferred
  Of him Thy name that fears.
6 Long life Thou to the king
      wilt give;
  Through generations he shall live,
  From age to age his years.

7 Before his God he shall abide;
  O do Thou truth and
      grace provide
  To keep him in the way.
8 So I Thy name will ever sing,
  A song of praise will daily bring,
  That I my vows may pay.

TUNE: JEHOVAH NISSI 886.886. (33B)
("Fear Not, O Little Flock") or
MERIBAH (33C)

Based on the *Book of Psalms,* 1871 and
The Psalter, 1912

49

Psalm 62

Verses 1–7

1 My soul in silence waits for God;
2 He's my salvation proved.
   He is my stronghold and my rock;
   I'll not be greatly moved.

3 How long will ye a man assail
   And seek to make him fall
   As though he were a
       tott'ring fence
   Or like a leaning wall?

4 They plot to bring his glory down;
   In lies they take delight;
   And while they bless him with
       their mouth,
   They curse with inward spite.

5 My soul, in silence wait for God,
   For He my hope has proved.
6 He's my salvation, stronghold,
       rock,
   And I shall not be moved.

7 In God alone my glory is
   And my salvation sure;
   My rock of strength is found
       in God,
   My refuge most secure.

Verses 8–12

8 On Him, O people, ever more
   Rely with confidence;
   Before Him pour ye out
       your heart,
   For God is our defense.

9 The sons of man are vanity,
   The best of men a lie;
   Together in the balance they
   Are lighter than a sigh.

10 Then in oppression do not hope;
   Nor yet for plunder lust;
   Though power and force may
       seem to thrive,
   In this build not your trust.

11 For truly God has spoken once;
   He twice to me made known:
   That strength and power belong
       to God
   And unto Him alone;

12 For so it is that sovereign grace
   Belongs to Thee, my Lord;
   For Thou according to his work
   Dost every man reward.

TUNE: ST. FLAVIAN CM (44B)
("In Sweet Communion, Lord")

Elements from *The Psalter,* 1912

Psalm 63

1 God, Thee, my God,
   I'll early seek;
   My soul's athirst for Thee.
   On dry land, weary, waterless,
   My flesh has longed for Thee.
2 Thus have I looked for
   Thee before
   Within Thy holy place
   That there I might behold
   Thy strength
   And glory of Thy face.

3 Because Thy grace is more
   than life
   My lips Thee praise shall give;
4 I in Thy name will lift my hands
   And bless Thee while I live.
5 My soul with rich, abundant food
   Shall be well satisfied;
   With shouts of joy upon my lips
   My mouth shall praise provide.

6 And when I turn my thought
   to Thee
   Upon my bed at night,
   As watches pass I meditate
   On Thee with great delight.
7 Thou art my help; I sing for joy
   In shadow of Thy wings.
8 For Thy right hand has held
   me fast;
   To Thee my spirit clings.

9 But they go down to depths
   of earth
   Who would my soul destroy;
10 They are delivered to the sword
   For jackals to enjoy.
11 The king shall then rejoice in God
   And all that by Him swear;
   For stopped shall be the mouths
   of those
   Who do a lie declare.

TUNE: ST. COLUMBA CM
(new *Trinity Hymnal*, p. 469)
("How Sweet and Awful Is the Place")

Psalm 64

First Version

1 Hear Thou my voice, O God,
   when I
   Make my complaint to Thee;
   From terror of the enemy
   Do Thou my life keep free.
2 Hide me from secret plots of men
   That evildoers be,
   From throng and tumult of the men
   That work iniquity.

3 Their tongues they have
   already whet
   To make them sharp as swords;
   And as their arrows they
   have aimed
   Their sharp and bitter words,
4 That they may at the innocent
   From ambush aim their shot;
   They without warning shoot
   at him,
   And, feeling safe, fear not.

5 In all their evil purposes
   They bid themselves be bold;
   They talk of laying hidden snares,
   And say, "Who shall behold?"
6 They have devised injustices;
   A cunning plot they keep;
   Because the inward thought of man,
   His very heart, is deep.

7 But God will shoot a shaft at them
   And wound them suddenly;
8 For their own tongue shall them
   confound,
   And all who see shall flee.
9 And then all men will stand in awe,
   The work of God declare;
   And they will thoughtfully observe
   What these his doings are.

10 The righteous in the Lord will joy,
   In Him will refuge take;
   And all who are upright in heart
   Will boasts of triumph make.

TUNE: CULROSS CM (64A)

51

Psalm 64

Second Version

1 Hear my voice, O God in
my complaint;
Guard my life from terror
of the foe.
2 Hide me from the plots of
wicked men,
From the noisy mob of evil ones,
3 Men who whet their tongues as
sharp as swords,
Who like arrows aim their
bitter words,
4 Shoot from ambush at the innocent
Without warning, with no fear
of harm.

5 They agree to form an evil plot;
Secretly they talk of laying snares,
Saying, "Who shall see them
or detect?"
6 They plan carefully their
wicked schemes;
They are ready with a
cunning plot;
For man's inward thought and
heart are deep.
7 God will shoot an arrow straight
at them;
Without warning they will
wounded be.

8 They will all be made to
trip themselves;
They'll undo themselves by
their own tongue.
All who see them then shall
shake their heads.
9 Then shall all men living be afraid,
Publish what God does and
learn His work.
10 In the LORD the righteous shall
be glad;
He will always put his trust
in Him.
All the right in heart will
boast with joy.

TUNE: SCHMÜCKE DICH 99.99.D (64B)

Psalm 65

Verses 1–5

1 Praise waits for Thee in Zion!
To Thee vows paid shall be.
2 O God, of prayer the hearer,
All flesh shall come to Thee.
3 Iniquities are daily
Prevailing over me,
But all of our transgressions
Are covered o'er by Thee.

4 How blessed the man
Thou choosest
And bringest near to Thee,
That in Thy courts forever
His dwelling place may be.
We shall within Thy temple
Be wholly satisfied
And filled with all the goodness
Thy sacred courts provide.

5 O God of our salvation,
Thou in Thy righteousness
With awesome deeds
and wonders
Thine answer wilt express,
O Thou in Whom confiding
All ends of earth agree,
And people who are sailing
Upon the farthest sea.

Verses 6–13

6 Thy might has built the moun-
tains;
Power clothes Thee evermore,
7 To calm the nations' clamor
And still the ocean's roar.
8 Thine awesome signs
and wonders
Fill distant lands with fear.
Thou makest dawn and sunset
For joy to shout and cheer.

9 Thy visits bring the showers;
Thou dost enrich the field.
God's river brims with water;
Thou dost prepare earth's yield.
10 Thou waterest earth's furrows;

52

Clods break down 'neath Thy rain.
Thou soft'nest earth with showers,
To bless each sprouting grain.

11 Thou crownest years with
      goodness;
   Thy steps enrich the ground.
12 The desert pastures blossom;
   The hills with joy resound.
13 The fields with flocks are covered;
   The vales with grain are clad.
   They all rejoice with shouting!
   They all with songs are glad!

TUNE: WEBB 76.76.D (65A)
("Stand Up, Stand Up for Jesus")

Based on the *Book of Psalms*, 1871 and
The Psalter, 1912

Psalm 66

Verses 1–6

1 All lands to God in joyful sounds
   Aloft your voices raise;
2 Sing forth the honor of His name,
   And glorious make His praise,
   And glorious make His praise.

3 Say unto God, How terrible
   In all Thy works art Thou!
   Through Thy great power Thy
      foes to Thee
   Shall be constrained to bow,
   Shall be constrained to bow.

4 Yes, all the earth shall
      worship Thee,
   And unto Thee shall sing;
   And to Thy name most glo-ri-ous
   Their songs of praise shall bring,
   Their songs of praise shall bring.

5 O come, behold the works
      of God,
   His mighty doings see;
   In dealing with the sons of men

Most terrible is He,
Most terrible is He.

   He turned the sea into dry land,
   So they a pathway had;
6 They through the river went
      on foot;
   There we in Him were glad,
   There we in Him were glad.

Verses 7–12

   He ruleth ever by His might;
   His eyes the nations try;
7 Let not the proud rebellious ones
   Exalt themselves on high,
   Exalt themselves on high.

   O all ye people, bless our God;
   Aloud proclaim His praise,
8 Who holdeth safe our soul in life,
   Our feet from sliding stays,
9 Our feet from sliding stays.

   For Thou, O God, hast tested us
   As silver is refined;
10 Didst take us in a net; on us
   A heavy load didst bind,
11 A heavy load didst bind.

   Thou madest men ride
      o'er our heads;
12 Through fire and flood we passed;
   But Thou didst bring us out
      to share
   A bounteous place at last,
   A bounteous place at last.

(Turn page for next section)

Verses 13–20

I'll bring burnt off'rings to
   Thy house;
13 To Thee my vows will pay,
As I gave promise with my lips
When trouble on me lay,
14 When trouble on me lay.

Burnt sacrifice of fattened beasts
With smoke of rams I'll take,
15 And from the bullocks and
   the goats
To Thee an off'ring make,
To Thee an off'ring make.

All ye that fear Him, come
   and hear
16 What God did for my soul;
I with my mouth have cried
   to Him;
17 My tongue did Him extol,
My tongue did Him extol.

18 If in my heart I sin regard,
The Lord will never hear;
19 But surely God has heard
   my voice;
He to my prayer gave ear,
He to my prayer gave ear.

20 Forever bless-ed be our God;
My prayer He has not spurned,
Nor has He ever yet from me
His lovingkindness turned,
His lovingkindness turned.

TUNE: MILES LANE CM (66A)
("All Lands to God")

Based on *Scottish Psalter*, 1650,
the *Book of Psalms*, 1871
and *The Psalter*, 1912

Psalm 67

1 O God, to us show mercy,
And bless us in Thy grace;
Cause Thou to shine upon us
The brightness of Thy face;
2 That so Thy way most holy
On earth may soon be known,
And unto ev'ry people
Thy saving grace be shown.

3 O God, let peoples praise Thee;
Let all the people sing;
4 Let nations now be joyful;
Let songs of gladness ring;
For Thou wilt judge the peoples
In truth and righteousness;
And o'er the earth shall nations
Thy leadership confess.

5 O God, let peoples praise Thee;
Let all the people sing;
6 For earth in rich abundance
To us her fruit will bring.
God, our own God, will bless us;
Yea, God will blessing send;
And all the earth shall fear Him
To its remotest end.

TUNE: MISSIONARY HYMN 76.76.D
(67A)
("From Greenland's Icy Mountains")

Based on the *Book of Psalms*, 1871,
and *The Psalter*, 1912

54

Psalm 68

Verses 1 8

1 Let God arise, and scattered far
  Be all His enemies;
  And let all those who do Him hate
  Before His presence flee,
2 As smoke is driven, drive Thou
    them;
  As wax melts by the fire,
  Let wicked men before God's face
  So perish in His ire.

3 But let all righteous men be glad;
  Let them before God's sight
  Be very joyful; yea, let them
  Rejoice with all their might.
4 Sing praise to God; prepare
    His way;
  Jehovah is His name,
  Who rideth through the wilder-
    ness;
  Before Him joy proclaim.

5 He takes a father's place to those
  Who are left fatherless;
  The widow's judge is God, within
  His place of holiness.
6 Yea, God the solitary sets
  In families; from bands
  The chained doth free; but
    rebels do
  Inhabit desert lands.

7 O God, the time Thy going forth
  Was at Thy people's head,
  The time when Thy
    majestic march
  Into the desert led,
8 Then at God's presence
    trembled earth;
  The melting heavens fell;
  This Sinai quaked, for God
    was there,
  The God of Is-ra-el.

9 A shower of fresh, abundant rain,
  O God, Thou sendest then;
  Thine heritage, when it was faint,
  Thou didst revive again.
10 Thy congregation found
    their home;
  Thy people settled there.
  O God, Thou with Thy
    goodness didst
  For all the poor prepare.

11 The LORD will give the word
    which He
  Commanded to be shown;
  The women are a mighty host
  To make the tidings known.
12 The kings of mighty hosts
    shall flee,
  Shall flee in haste away;
  And she that tarried at her house
  Will then divide the prey.

13 Though ye may lie in cattle pens,
  Ye shall yourselves enfold
  In silver feathers, like a dove
  With wings of brilliant gold.
14 There as th'Almighty scattered
    kings
  On Zalmon fell the snow.
15 God's mountain is the
    Bashan range
  With lofty peaks to show.

16 Why look askance, ye mountain
    peaks,
  Upon the holy hill
  Where God the LORD desires
    to dwell?
  Yes, He forever will!
17 God's chariots twenty thousand
    are,
  Yes, thousands multiplied.
  The Lord's among them, as
    He was
  On Sinai's mountainside.

(Continues)

55

18 Thou didst ascend on high and lead
   captivity away,
   Received ev'n rebels' gifts, that God
   The LORD might with them stay.
19 O bless-ed be the Lord, Who doth
   Each day our burden bear;
   He our salvation is alone;
   He, God, for us will care.

Verses 20–27

20 Our God is unto us a God
   Who brings de-liv-er-ance,
   And unto us escape from death
   The Lord Jehovah grants.
21 But surely God shall wound
      the head
   Of those that are His foes.
   He'll seize the scalp of him that on
   In guilt and trespass goes.

22 The Lord has said, "From
      Bashan range
   I will bring back these foes,
   I will bring back my enemies
   Which ocean's depths enclose,
   That thou mayst dip thy foot
23   in blood,
   That thy dog's tongue may share
   It's portion of thine enemies
   By Me defeated there."

24 They saw Thy great procession,
      God,
   The great procession's pace,
   Directed by my God, my King,
   In holiness and grace.
25 Before went singers; after them
   The minstrels music made,
   And bands of maidens all around
   Their ringing timbrels played.

26 Within the congregations all
   Bless God with one accord;
   All ye who come from
      Israel's fount,
   O do ye bless the LORD.
27 Their prince, young Benjamin,
      is there,
   And Judah's princes high;
   The chiefs of Zebulon are there,
   And those of Naphtali.

Verses 28–35

28 Thy God commands thy strength;
      for us
   Thy work, God, strengthened be.
29 For Thy house in Jerusalem
   Let kings bring gifts to thee.
30 Rebuke the beasts among the
      reeds,
   Those trampling bulls of might,
   With all the other peoples who
   But calves are in their sight,

   That all may humbly bow
      themselves,
   Bring bars of silver ore.
   For He has scattered peoples all
   Who take delight in war.
31 Then shall the princes proud
      and great
   Come out of Egypt's lands,
   And Ethiopia to God
   Shall soon stretch forth her hands.

32 O all ye kingdoms of the earth,
   Sing praises unto God;
   And Him who is the Lord of all
   With praises do ye laud
33 To Him that rides on heav'n of
      heav'ns
   Which He of old did found;
   Lo' He sends out His voice, a voice
   In might that doth abound.

34 All strength to God do ye ascribe,
   Because His majesty
   Is over Is-ra-el; His strength
   Is in the heavens high.
35 Thou, God, are dreadful from
      Thy place;
   Isr'el's own God is He,
   Who gives His people strength and
      power;
   O let God bless-ed be.

TUNE: WEYMOUTH CMD (68D)

Based on *Scottish Psalter*, 1650;
vv. 1–6, *The Book of Psalms
with Music*, 1950

Psalm 69

Verses 1–9

1 Save me, O God, because
    the floods
  Come in upon my soul;
2 I sink in mire where none
    can stand;
  Deep waters o'er me roll.
3 I with my crying weary am;
  My throat is parched and dried;
  My eyes grow dim while for
    my God
  Still waiting I abide.

4 The men that with no cause at all
  Bear hatred unto me
  More than the hairs upon
    my head
  In number seem to be.
  Those wrongfully my enemies
  Who seek my soul to slay
  Are very strong; I must restore
  What I took not away.

5 O God, my foolishness and sins
  Are surely known to Thee.
6 Let none that wait on Thee
    be shamed,
  Lord GOD of hosts, through me.
  O Thou, the God of Is-ra-el,
  Let none that seek Thy face
  Be ever made to suffer shame
  For my acts of disgrace.

7 For I have borne reproach
    for Thee;
  My face is veiled with shame.
8 To brothers strange, to mother's
    sons
  An alien, I became.
9 For zeal within me for Thy house
  Has been consuming me,
  And all reproaches cast at Thee
  Have fallen now on me.

Verses 10–19

10 When I was weeping in my soul,
   My fasting was my shame;
11 When I in sackcloth
    clothed myself,
   Their byword I became.
12 The men who sit within the gate
   Have talked about me long;
   And those who gave themselves
    to drink
   About me made a song.

13 But in a time accepted, LORD,
   To Thee my prayers ascend;
   In Thine abounding love
    and truth,
   O God, salvation send.
14 Deliver me from out the mire,
   And me from sinking keep;
   Deliver me from those that hate,
   And from the waters deep.

15 Let not the flood me overflow;
   Let me not swallowed be
   By gaping deep; let not the pit
   Close up its mouth on me.
16 Because Thy mercy, LORD, is good,
   O answer Thou my plea;
   In all of Thy compassion great,
   O turn Thou unto me.

17 Ne'er from Thy servant hide
    Thy face;
   I'm pressed; soon answer me.
18 Draw near to me; redeem
    my soul;
   My foes come; ransom me.
19 Well known to Thee is my
    reproach,
   My shame and my disgrace;
   The adversaries of my soul
   Are all before Thy face.

(Turn page for next section)

Verses 20–29

20 My heart is broken by reproach,
   And I am sick and weak.
   I never find the sympathy
   And comforters I seek.
21 They also gave me bitter gall
   In all the food I ate;
   They gave me vinegar to drink
   The time my thirst was great.

22 O let their peace become a trap;
   A snare their table make;
23 In darkness let their eyesight fail,
   And cause their loins to shake.
24 On them Thine indignation pour;
   In wrath them overtake;
25 And let their camp be desolate;
   Their tents let all forsake.

26 For they have persecuted him
   Whom Thou Thyself didst smite;
   They advertise the pain of those
   On whom Thy wounds did light.
27 Keep adding their iniquities;
   Sum up their wickedness;
   And let them never enter in
   To share Thy righteousness.

28 And from the record book of life
   O let them be erased;
   Upon the roll of righteous men
   Let not their names be placed.
29 But as for me, afflicted, poor,
   And deep in pain am I;
   By Thy salvation, O my God,
   Let me be set on high.

Verses 30–36

30 The name of God I with a song
   Most cheerfully will praise;
   And I in giving thanks to Him
   His name will highly raise.
31 For this will please the LORD
      far more
   Than will the offering
   Of any ox with horns and hoofs,
   Or bullock, which I bring.

32 The humble ones have seen
      all this,
   And are with gladness thrilled.
   All ye who seek for God, O let
   Your heart with life be filled.
33 Because Jehovah hears
      the prayers
   That from the needy rise,
   And those that are His pris-on-ers
   He never will despise.

34 Let heav'n and earth give praise,
      and all
   With which the sea is filled;
35 For God will Zion surely save,
   And Judah's cities build.
   They'll dwell in their inheritance,
36 Their children's heritage;
   His servants, those who love
      His name,
   Dwell there from age to age.

TUNE: BEATITUDO CM (90B)
("O for a Closer Walk") or
MAPLE AVENUE CMD
(*Psalter Hymnal* [4th ed.], p. 14)

Based on *Scottish Psalter*, 1650

Psalm 70

1 O God, deliver me.
  LORD, speed Your help to me;
2 And let all those who seek
    my soul
  Ashamed and humbled be.

  Turned back be they, disgraced,
  That in my hurt delight;
3 Appalled by their own shame
    be they
  Who say, "Aha", in spite.

4 Let all who seek Thee joy
  And glad in Thee abide.
  Let those who Thy salvation love
  Say, "God be magnified."

5 In need am I and poor;
  O God, make haste I pray;
  My help and my Deliverer,
  O LORD, do not delay.

TUNE: STATE STREET SM (70B)
("Behold the Throne of Grace")

Elements from *Scottish Psalter*, 1650, and
  The Psalter, 1912

Psalm 71

Verses 1–14

1 O LORD, in Thee I'm trusting;
  Ashamed let me not be;
2 O save me in Thy righteousness,
  Give ear, and rescue me.
3 Be Thou my rock, my
    dwelling place,
  My constant safe resort.
  Thou my salvation hast ordained;
  Thou art my rock and fort.

4 From wicked hands, God,
    free me,
  Hands cru-el and unjust;
5 Thou, Lord Jehovah, art my hope;
  From youth Thou art my trust.
6 For I have been sustained
    by Thee
  Through birth and early days;
  Brought from my mother's womb
    by Thee,
  I'll give Thee constant praise.

7 To many I'm a wonder;
  Thou art my refuge strong.
8 My mouth is brimming with
    Thy praise
  And honor all day long.
9 Do not reject me in the time
  When old age I shall see;
  And in my days of failing strength
  Do not abandon me.

10 My enemies with hatred
   Against me evil speak;
   Those who are watching for
     my life
   United counsel seek.
11 They say, "God has forsaken him!
   Pursue him! None will save!"
12 O God, do not be far from me;
   My God, Thy help I crave.

13 Let all who strive against me
   Disgraced and wasted be,
   All covered with reproach
     and shame
   Who seek to injure me.
14 But I with lasting confidence
   Will hope con-tin-ual-ly,
   And I will add still more and more
   To all the praise of Thee.

(Turn page for next section)

Verses 15–24, 1

15 All day my mouth Thy justice
   And Thy salvation show,
   For proofs of them are far beyond
16 The numbers which I know.
   For I will go forth in the strength
   Of Thee, Jehovah Lord;
   Thy righteousness, and Thine
        alone,
   Abroad I will record.

17 O God, You've been my teacher
   Ev'n from my days of youth;
   And all the wonders Thou
        hast done
   I still declare as truth.
18 So now, when I am old and gray,
   O God, forsake me not,
   Until Thy strength and power   .
        I have
   Each generation taught.

19 For, God, Thy justice reaches
   Into infinity,
   And Thou hast wrought such
        miracles,
   O God, who is like Thee?
20 Thou Who before hast made
        me see
   Much evil and distress
   Wilt me revive and bring me up
   From depths which me depress.

21 Do Thou increase my greatness,
   And comfort to me bring.
22 Then with a harp I'll give Thee
        thanks;
   My God, Thy truth I'll sing.
   O Holy One of Is-ra-el,
   With harp Thy psalms I'll bring;
23 My lips will shout; my ransomed
        soul
   In psalms to Thee will sing.

24 My tongue will keep proclaiming
   Thy justice all day long;
   For they are humbled and
        ashamed
   Who seek to do me wrong.

1 O Lord, in Thee I refuge take;
   Ashamed let me not be;
   O save me in Thy righteousness;
   Give ear and rescue me.

TUNE: ST. CHRISTOPHER 76.86.86.86.
   (new *Trinity Hymnal*, p. 251)
   ("Beneath the Cross of Jesus")

Based on *The Psalter*, 1912; altered 1994

Psalm 72

Verses 1–12

1 O God, Thy judgments give
        the king,
   His reigning son Thy
        righteousness;
2 He to Thy people right
        shall bring,
   With justice shall Thy
        poor redress.
3 The heights shall bring prosperity,
   The hills bring peace by
        righteousness;
4 He'll judge the poor,
        the wronged set free,
   And crush the men who
        them oppress.

5 Till sun and moon no more
        are known
   They shall Thee fear in ages all;
6 He'll come as rain on meadows
        mown
   And show'rs upon the earth
        that fall.
7 The just shall flourish in his day;
   While lasts the moon shall
        peace extend;
8 From sea to sea shall be his sway,
   And from the River to earth's end.

9 The nomads bow to him as king,
   And to the dust his foes descend;
10 The isles and Tarshish
        tribute bring,
   And Sheba, Seba gifts shall send.

60

11 All kings shall down before
        him fall,
   All nations his commands obey.
12 He'll save the needy when
        they call,
   The poor, and those that have
        no stay.

Verses 13–19

13 He'll show the poor his sympathy,
   And save the needy by his might;
14 From fraud and force he'll set
        them free;
   Their blood is precious in
        his sight.
15 So he shall live; a gift of gold
   From Sheba they'll before him lay.
   They'll him in constant
        prayer uphold,
   Their blessings on him
        chant all day.

16 On hilltops sown a little grain,
   Like Lebanon with fruit
        shall bend;
   New life the city shall attain;
   She shall like grass grow
        and extend.
17 Long as the sun his name
        shall last.
   It shall endure through ages all;
   And men shall still in him
        be bless'd;
   Bless'd all the nations shall
        him call.

18 Now bless-ed be our God alone.
   Jehovah, God of Is-ra-el;
   For only He has wonders done;
   His deeds in glory far excel.
19 And bless-ed be His
        glorious name,
   Long as the ages shall endure.
   O'er all the earth extend His fame;
   Amen, amen, for evermore.

TUNE: TRURO LM (72A)
("Lift Up Your Head, Ye Mighty Gates")

Based on the *Book of Psalms*, 1871

Psalm 73

Verses 1–16

1 God's surely good to Is-ra-el,
   To every one whose heart is pure.
2 But as for me, I nearly fell;
   My footsteps were no longer sure.
3 For I was envious of the proud
   And wicked ones with
        wealth endowed.

4 For in their death no
        pangs they know;
   Their strength is firm from
        day to day;
5 They have no part in others' woe,
   Nor plagued as mortal men
        are they.
6 They make their necklace
        arrogance,
   And clothe themselves
        with violence.

7 Their eyes are bulging
        from excess;
   Their hearts o'erflow with
        dreams they seek.
8 They scoff; they threaten
        to oppress;
   Disdainful words they
        proudly speak.
9 Their mouth the heights of
        heaven raids;
   Their tongue around the world
        parades.

10 Their people therefore
        this way turn
   And drink their streams
        that overflow.
11 "For how," they say, "can God
        discern?
   And does the Most High
        really know?"
12 Behold, ungodly men are these,
   Who gain in wealth and
        live at ease.

(Continues)

61

13 Then surely I have toiled in vain
   To cleanse my heart from
      all offense,
   And vainly from each guilty stain
   Have washed my hands
      in innocence.
14 Still grievous plagues all day
      I've borne
   And have been chastened
      every morn.

15 If I would let my thoughts
      lead me
   To speak with doubting words
      this way,
   Behold, the children called
      by Thee
   I certainly would then betray.
16 But though the facts I tried to see
   The problem deeply troubled me.

Verses 17–28

17 Then came I to God's sanctu'ry
   And there considered well
      their end.
18 They're set on slipp'ry ground
      by Thee,
   And them to ruin Thou dost send.
19 How rapidly destroyed are they,
   By sudden terrors swept away!

20 As one who from a dream
      awakes,
   Their form, O Lord, Thou
      wilt despise.
21 So when my heart with
      grieving breaks,
   And bitter thoughts within
      me rise,
22 I senseless am, and blind within;
   A beast before Thee I have been.

23 Yet evermore I am with Thee:
   Thou holdest me by my
      right hand.
24 And Thou, ev'n Thou, my guide
      shalt be;
   Thy counsel shall my way
      command;

And afterward in glory bright
   Shalt Thou receive me to
      Thy sight.

25 For whom have I in heav'n
      but Thee?
   None else on earth I long
      to know.
26 My flesh may faint and weary be;
   My heart may fail and
      heavy grow;
   With strength doth God my
      heart restore;
   He is my portion evermore.

27 They perish that are far
      from Thee;
   Lo, in their lewdness they
      shall die.
28 But surely it is good for me
   That unto God I should
      draw nigh.
   I refuge take in GOD the Lord,
   That all Thy works I may record.

TUNE: MELITA 88.88.88. (84B)
("Eternal Father, Strong to Save") or
ST. PETERSBURG 88.88.88. (73B)

Psalm 74

Verses 1–11

1 Why, God, forever cast us off?
  Why does Your anger burn
  Against the flock of Your
    own field;
2 Recall Your congregation which
  You purchased from of old.

  Remember them that You
    redeemed,
  Your tribe and heritage,
  And Zion's mount where You
    did dwell.
3 O turn Your steps to walk about
  Where endless ruin is.

  Your foes laid waste the
    holy place;
4 They shouted in Your halls;
  They set their al-ien emblems up;
5 They swung their axes as if they
  Were clearing woods of trees.

6 With pikes they broke the
    carven work;
7 The holy place they burned.
  The place You made Your name
    to dwell,
  Now even to the very dust
  They have profaned and razed.

8 "O let us bring their strength
    to naught!"
  So did their hearts declare.
  They burned each God-appointed
    place.
9 There is no prophet now, no signs
  And none who knows how long.

10 How long, O God, will foes insult
  And scorn Your name always?
11 O why do You hold back
    Your hand?
  Why not stretch forth your strong
    right hand
  To end and to destroy.

Verses 12–23

12 Yet God my King brings forth
    of old
  Salvation in the earth.
13 The sea You parted by
    Your strength;
14 You crushed the fierce Leviathan
  And fed him to the beasts.

15 You opened springs; You dried
    the streams;
16 Both day and night are Yours
  You have ordained both light
    and sun;
17 You gave the earth its boundaries,
  And made the heat and cold.

18 Remember, LORD, how foes insult!
  How fools have scorned
    Your name!
19 Your dove O give not to
    the beasts!
  The company of your meek ones
  Do not always forget!

20 O look upon the covenant!
  The darkness of the land
  Is with the dens of plunder filled.
21 O do not shame the meek, but let
  The needy praise Your name!

22 Arise, O God! Take up Your strife!
  Recall the scorn of fools!
23 Recall Your adversaries cries,
  The raging uproar of your foes
  Which rises endlessly.

TUNE: REST 8.6.8.8.6.
(*The Hymnbook*, p. 416)
("Dear Lord and Father of Mankind")

Altered 1994

Psalm 75

1 To Thee, O God, we render
   thanks,
To Thee give thanks sincere,
Because Thy wondrous
   works declare
That Thy great name is near.
2 When my appointed time is come,
I'll judge with even hand.
3 Though earth and all its
   dwellers melt,
I make its pillars stand.

4 I to the boastful said, "Boast not!"
To vile men, "Lift no horn!
5 Do not lift up your horn on high,
Nor speak with neck of scorn!"
6 For not from east nor west
   nor wilds
Comes exaltation nigh,
7 For God is judge, debasing one,
Another raising high.

8 The LORD pours out a foaming cup
Which well-mixed wine contains,
And every wicked one on earth
Must drink; the dregs he drains.
9 But I will tell it evermore,
To Jacob's God sing praise;
10 And horns of sinners I'll cut off,
But just men's horns I'll raise.

TUNE: MEDFIELD (SHEFFIELD) CM
(16A)

Elements from *Scottish Psalter,* 1650
and *The Psalter,* 1912

Psalm 76

1 God the Lord is known in Judah;
Great His name in Is-ra-el;
2 His pavilion is in Salem;
His abode on Zion hill.
3 There he broke the bow
   and arrows,
Bade the sword and shield
   be still.

4 Excellent art Thou and glorious
Coming from the hills of prey.
5 Thou hast spoiled the
   valiant-hearted;
Wrapt in sleep of death are they.
Mighty men have lost
   their cunning;
None are ready for the fray.

6 Horse and char-iot low are lying
In the sleep of death's dark night.
Jacob's God, Thou didst
   rebuke them;
7 Thou art fearful in Thy might.
When Thine anger once is risen,
Who may stand before Thy sight?

8 When from heav'n Thy
   sentence sounded,
All the earth in fear was still,
9 While to save the meek and lowly
God in judgment wrought
   His will.
10 Ev'n the wrath of man shall
   praise Thee;
What remains is kept from ill.

11 Make your vows now to Jehovah;
Pay your God what is His own.
All men, bring your gifts
   before Him;
Fear is due to Him alone;
12 He brings low the pride
   of princes;
Kings shall tremble at His frown.

TUNE: NEANDER 87.87.87. (76A)
("Christ is Coming")

Elements from *The Psalter,* 1912

Psalm 77

Verses 1–10

1 With supplicating cry to God
   My voice shall lifted be;
   Yes, unto God I lift my voice,
   And He will answer me.
2 Through all the day I sought
      the Lord,
   When troubles on me pressed;
   Through all the night I
      stretched my hands;
   My soul refused to rest.

3 Again, as I remember God,
   Disquietness prevails;
   And as I deeply meditate,
   My sighing spirit fails.
4 For Thou hast held my eyelids so
   That they are open wide;
   Yet I so deeply troubled am
   To speak I have not tried.

5 I've thought on days and
      years gone by,
   Recalled my song at night;
6 I've meditated with my heart;
   My spirit searched for light.
7 Forever will the Lord cast off,
   Show favor never more?
8 Forever has His mercy gone?
   Will His word come no more?

9 Has God forgotten all His grace?
   Has His compassion gone?
   Or can it be His mercies all
   He has in wrath withdrawn?
10 Then I replied, "Such questions
      show
   My own infirmity.
   The firm right hand of Him
      Most High
   Through years must
      changeless be."

Verses 11–20

11 The Lord's deeds I remember will,
   Thy works of old recall.
12 I'll ponder all which Thou
      hast done
   And weigh Thy wonders all.
13 O God, most holy is Thy way;
   What god is like our God?
14 O God of miracles, Thy strength
   Thou hast made known abroad.

15 Thou hast redeemed Thy
      people all,
   The power of Thine arm shown.
   Thy people sons of Jacob are,
   And Joseph is Thine own.
16 The waters sighted Thee, O God;
   The waters sighted Thee.
   They were in anguish, and
      the deeps
   Then trembled fearfully.

17 Then from thick clouds the
      waters poured;
   A sound came from the sky.
   Thine arrows flashing here
      and there
   Abroad began to fly.
18 Amid the whirlwinds of the sky
   Thy voice in thunder pealed;
   Thy lightnings lightened up
      the world;
   The earth with trembling reeled.

19 Thy way was in the troubled sea,
   Thy path in waters deep.
   Thy footprints have remained
      unknown;
   None can their record keep.
20 Thy people like a flock of sheep
   Were led at Thy command,
   By Moses and by Aaron kept,
   And guided by their hand.

TUNE: EFFINGHAM CM (77C)
   or MYRA CMD (51B)

Psalm 78

Verses 1–8

1 O ye my people, to my law
   Attentively give ear;
   The words that from my
      mouth proceed
   Incline yourselves to hear.
2 My mouth shall speak a parable,
   The sayings dark of old,
3 Which we have listened to
      and known
   As by our fathers told.

4 We will not hide them
      from their sons
   But tell the race to come
   Jehovah's praises and His strength,
   The wonders He has done.
5 His word He unto Jacob gave,
   His law to Is-ra-el,
   And bade our fathers teach
      their sons
6 The coming race to tell,

   That children yet unborn
      might know
   And their descendants lead
7 To trust in God, recall
      God's works,
   And His commandments heed,
8 And not be like their fathers were,
   A race of stubborn mood,
   Which never would prepare
      its heart
   Nor keep its faith with God.

Verses 9–20

9 The sons of E-phra-im
      were armed;
   For bows they did not lack;
   But when the day of battle came,
   Fainthearted they turned back.
10 They did not keep God's
      covenant,
   Nor walk in his commands.
11 His wonders shown them
      they forgot,
   The deeds done by His hands.

12 Great miracles He brought to pass
   Before their fathers' sight;
   In Egypt's land, in Zoan's field
   He showed His wondrous might.
13 He split the sea to let them pass;
   The waters stood aside;
14 By day He led them with a cloud;
   All night a flame was guide.

15 He split the rocks and gave
      them drink,
   As from great deeps below;
16 He from the rock brought
      running streams,
   Like floods made waters flow.
17 Yet in the desert still they sinned,
   Provoking the most High;
18 For in their heart they tested God,
   Urged Him their lust supply.
19 They spoke against their God;
      they said,
   "Can even God provide
   A table in the wilderness
   That we may be supplied?
20 Behold, He struck the rock
      and out
   Gushed streams of water sweet;
   But can He give His people bread
   And send them flesh to eat?"

Verses 21–34

21 Because the LORD heard this,
      His wrath
   Was kindled into flame;
   On Jacob, and on Is-ra-el
   His indignation came.
22 For they did not believe in God
   Nor trust His saving love;
23 But still he opened heaven's
      doors,
   Commanded clouds above,

24 And rained His manna down
      on them;
   He gave them grain from heav'n;
25 And man partook of angels' food,
   In His abundance giv'n.

26 In heav'n He made the
  east wind blow;
 The south wind felt His hand;
27 So He rained meat on them
  like dust,
 Winged fowl like ocean's sand.

28 He let them fall amid their camp,
 By tents on every side.
29 And so they ate till they
  were filled;
 Their greed He satisfied.
30 They craved still more, mouths
  filled with food;
 God's wrath then on them fell
31 And killed their stout ones
  and subdued
 Choice men of Is-ra-el.

32 Yet still they sinned; they
  disbelieved
 His wonders in the way;
33 So in a breath He closed
  their days,
 Their years in deep dismay.
34 But when he killed them,
  they desired
 To seek Him eagerly;
 So they returned and searched
  for God
 With sense of urgency.

Verses 35–46

35 They then remembered God to be
 Their rock eternally,
 And knew that only God
  Most High
 Could their redeemer be.
36 But they enticed Him with
  their mouth,
 And with their tongue they lied;
37 Their heart was not sincere
  toward Him;
 His cov'nant they denied.

38 But He forgave iniquity
 In mercy, did not slay,
 Aroused not all His wrath, but oft

His anger turned away.
39 Thus he remembered they
  were flesh,
 That they were only men,
 A breath that swiftly goes away
 And never comes again.

40 How oft rebelled they in
  the wilds,
 Grieved Him 'neath desert sun!
41 They often tested God,
  brought pain
 On Isr'el's Holy One.
42 For they remembered not
  His hand,
 Nor kept in mind the day
 When He in power redeemed
  them from
 Their adversary's sway.

43 How He in Egypt wonders did
 And signs in Zoan's field;
 He turned their rivers into blood;
44 Their streams no drink
  would yield.
45 He sent de-vour-ing swarms of flies,
 And frogs their land to spoil;
46 To grasshoppers He gave
  their crops,
 To locusts all their toil.

(Turn page for next section)

67

Verses 47–55

47 He killed their tender vines
    with hail,
    Their sycamores with frost;
48 He smote their flocks with
    thunderbolts;
    In hail their herds were lost.
49 His heat of anger, fury, woe,
    And indignation burned;
    All these upon them He as His
    Destroying angels turned.

50 He for His anger smoothed a path,
    Spared not their soul from death;
    But as a prey to pestilence
    He gave away their breath.
51 And over Egypt's land He smote
    Their firstborn sons, their pride,
    Until in all the tents of Ham
    Their chief of strength had died.

52 But His own people forth
    like sheep
    He brought with guiding hand,
    And led his people like a flock
    Across the desert land.
53 He led them safely, that no fear
    Among them might be found,
    But in the overwhelming sea
    Their enemies were drowned.

54 He brought them through
    the boundary
    Into His holy land,
    This very mountain which He had
    Possessed by His right hand.
55 Before them he drove nations out,
    Gave them inheritance
    By measured lot, caused
    Isr'el's tribes
    To dwell within their tents.

Verses 56–62

56 And yet they tempted God
    Most High,
    Rebelled against His will;
    The testimonies He proclaimed
    They disregarded still.

57 They like their fathers
    backward turned
    In treachery and pride;
    Like shafts from a deceitful bow
    They all did turn aside.

58 With their high places they
    to wrath
    Provoked Him constantly;
    And with their graven images
    Aroused His jealousy.
59 God heard, and in His anger great
    Rejected Isr'el then;
60 The tent at Shiloh He forsook
    Where He had dwelt with men.

61 So he delivered up His strength
    Into captivity,
    His glory gave into the hand
    Of His proud enemy.
62 And He His people to the sword
    Delivered to be killed.
    Against His own inheritance
    With anger he was filled.

Verses 63–72, 1

63 Their young men were devoured
    by fire;
    Their maidens were unwed;
64 And when their priests fell by
    the sword
    No tears their widows shed.
65 The Lord awoke as from a sleep,
    Like warrior cheered by wine;
66 He drove His adversaries back,
    Made their reproach a sign.

67 Then Joseph's tent rejected He,
    On Ephraim would not count;
68 But He the tribe of Judah chose,
    For He loved Zion's Mount.
69 And there exalted like the heights
    He built His sanctu'ry,
    And like the earth He founded it
    For all eternity.

70 He for His servant David chose,
    Took him from guarding sheep,
71 Brought him from where the ewes
    and lambs

It was his task to keep,
That He might shepherd
   Jacob then
And lead His people well,
Watch over His inheritance,
His chosen Is-ra-el.

72 So with integrity of heart
Them faithfully he fed,
And with his understanding hands
He guided as he led.
1 O ye my people, to my law
Attentively give ear;
The words that from my
   mouth proceed
Incline yourselves to hear.

TUNE: ELLACOMBE CMD (78C)
("Hosanna, Loud Hosanna")

Elements from *Scottish Psalter,* 1650

Psalm 79

Verses 1–7

1 God, into Thy holy temple
Heathen hordes have
   entrance made.
They defiled Thy house,
   and Salem
They in ruins laid.
2 They have cast Thy
   servants' bodies
To the fowls of heav'n for meat;
Flesh of Thy dear saints
   they've given
To wild beasts to eat.

3 Round Jerusalem like water
They Thy servants' blood
   have shed.
There was no one there to bury
Bodies of the dead.
4 We've become to all
   our neighbors
A derision and reproach.
We are scorned by those who,
   laughing,
On us now encroach.

5 LORD, how long wilt Thou
   be angry?
Will Thy wrath forever burn?
Will Thy blazing, jealous anger
Firelike on us turn?
6 Pour Thy wrath on heathen
   kingdoms
Who know not nor call Thy
   name,
7 Who devour and swallow Jacob,
Waste His land in flame.

Verses 8–13

8 Count not sins of all our fathers
Which upon us guilt bestow;
Let Thy mercy rush to meet us,
Now brought very low.
9 God of our salvation, help us!
To Thy name the glory take.
Rescue us! Our sins forgive us
For Thine own name's sake.

10 "Where's their God?" exclaim
   the nations.
Make them with us see instead
How Thou justly art avenging
Blood Thy servants shed.
11 O let pris'ners' sighs ascending
Come before Thee there on high.
By Thy mighty power
   preserve them
Who are doomed to die.

12 Back into our neighbors' bosom
Turn a sevenfold reward
For reproaches they've
   been casting
On Thee, O my Lord.
13 We Thy flock of sheep,
   Thy people,
Ever to Thee thanks will raise.
On through every generation
We proclaim Thy praise.

TUNE: ST. LEONARD 87.85.
(new *Trinity Hymnal,* p. 644)
("May the Mind of Christ My Savior")

Elements from *Scottish Psalter,* 1650

Psalm 80

1 Hear, O hear us, Is-rael's
   Shepherd,
  Who drives forth Joseph like
   a flock!
  From the cherubim, O shine forth!
  Rise in valor that we be saved!
2 So arise in sight of Ephr'im,
  And Manasseh and Benjamin!
3 God, we pray, O turn us!
   Bring us back!
  Make Your face shine,
   and we are saved!

4 O how long, LORD God of Armies,
  Burns Your wrath at your
   people's prayer!
5 With the bread of tears You
   feed them,
  And full measure of tears
   they drink!
6 Strife you make us to our
   neighbors,
  And our foes laugh at us in scorn!
7 God of Armies, turn us!
   Bring us back!
  Make Your face shine,
   and we are saved!

8 You brought forth a vine
   from Egypt,
  And to plant it drove nations out.
9 You made room to root it deeply,
  And it flourished and filled
   the land.
10 Then its shadow wrapped
   the mountains,
  And its boughs hid the cedars tall!
11 To the sea it thrust great
   branches forth.
  And young shoots to the
   mighty stream!

12 Why have You torn down
   its fences?
  It is plucked by each
   passing hand!
13 Forest boars have gnawed
   upon it,

And wild creatures have
   pastured there!
14 Turn again, O God of Armies!
  Look from heav'n! Visit this
   Your vine!
15 So uphold what Your right hand
   did plant,
  And the son You raised up
   in strength!

16 It is burned and hewn in pieces
  By Your frown will they
   be destroyed!
17 Lay Your hand on him
   You favored,
  Son of man that You raised
   in strength!
18 Then from You we will
   not wander;
  Make us live! We will call
   Your name!
19 O LORD God of Armies,
   turn us back!
  Make Your face shine,
   and we are saved!

TUNE: BRYN CALFARIA 88.88.88.98. (80B)

Psalm 81

1 To God our Strength,
   to Jacob's God,
  A song and shout now raise!
2 With psalm and timbrel, harp,
   and lute,
  Awake to joyous praise!
3 At each new moon the
   trumpets blow
  For solemn festal days.

4 This is the law of Jacob's God,
  For Isr'el His command.
5 This witness He for Joseph set
  When smiting Egypt's land.
  When there I heard
   a foreign tongue
  I could not understand.

6 I from his shoulder took the load,
  His hands from burdens freed.
7 You called Me when in
   trouble sore;
  I saved you in your need,
  Tried you at streams of Meribah;
  In thunder I gave heed.

8 Hear, O my people! Is-ra-el:
  'Gainst you I'll testify.
  If only you would hear Me now!
9 On no strange god rely;
  Have none near you; don't
   worship them.
10 The LORD your God am I.

  I brought you up from
   Egypt's land;
  Your opened mouth I'll fill.
11 My people would not hear
   My voice;
  My Isr'el spurned me still.
12 I left them to their stubborn heart,
  To walk by their own will.

13 O that My people would Me hear
  And Isr'el choose My way!
14 How soon I would their
   foes subdue!
  My outstretched hand I'd lay
  Upon their adversaries all,
  To fill them with dismay.

15 Then all who hate the LORD
   would cringe,
16 In fear and dread abide.
  But Isr'el with the finest wheat
  He'd always keep supplied.
  And I with honey from the rock
  Would keep you satisfied.

TUNE: BROTHER JAMES AIR 86.86.86.
("The Lord's My Shepherd")
(new *Trinity Hymnal*, p. 86)

Psalm 82

1 God is in His congregation;
  Judge among the gods He stands.
2 How long will you judge unjustly,
  Favoring the wicked hands?

3 Judge the destitute and orphan,
  And the poor, distressed defend;
4 Free the destitute and needy;
  Save them from the
   wicked's hand.

5 These are they who have
   no knowledge,
  To perceive no effort make;
  They walk on in utter darkness;
  All of earth's foundations shake.

6 Gods you are, I have declared it,
  Sons now of the Highest, all;
7 Yet you'll die as common men die
  And like any prince shall fall.

8 Now, O God, arise we pray You,
  And the earth to judgment call;
  For You, as Your own possession,
  Shall inherit nations all.

TUNE: OMNI DIE 87.87. (82)

Psalm 83

1 Do not be silent, God,
   or unresponding!
Do not remain at rest,
   O Mighty One!
2 For now Your foes arouse and
   make a clamor;
Your bitter enemies lift up
   the head.
3 Against Your people now they
   plot in secret;
They meet to work against Your
   hidden ones.
4 They say, "Let us go up and
   end their nation.
The name of Is-ra-el shall be
   no more!"

5 Together they conspire in
   deadly earnest;
Against You they have made
   a covenant.
6 The Ish-mael-ites are there,
   the tents of Edom,
The men of Moab with
   the Hagarenes.
7 See Gebal, Amalek, with men
   of Ammon;
Behold Philistia and them of Tyre.
8 For Ashur too has come and joins
   their forces;
They are the pow-er of the sons
   of Lot.

9 Treat them like Midian,
   like Jabin's army.
Treat them like Sisera at Kishon's
   brook.
10 At Endor they were all
   annihilated,
And they became as dung upon
   the ground.
11 Like Oreb make their chiefs, Their
   lords like Zebah!
12 Who thought they would possess
   the land of God.
13 My God, O make them be like
   whirling dustclouds;
Make them like bits of chaff
   before the wind.

14 Like fire that burns the woods,
   like flames of lightning,
15 Pursue them with Your storms
   and strike with fear.
16 Fill up their faces with
   humiliation,
And let them seek Your name,
   Jehovah, then.
17 Let them be terrified and
   shamed forever,
And let them be dismayed and
   be destroyed!
Let them know You alone
   You are Jehovah
You are the One Most High
   o'er all the earth.

TUNE: SALVUM FAC 11.10.11.10.D
(83C)

Psalm 84

1 O LORD of hosts, how lovely
   The place where Thou dost dwell.
Thy tabernacles holy
   In pleasantness excel.
2 My soul is longing, fainting,
   Jehovah's courts to see;
My heart and flesh are crying,
   O living God, for Thee.

3 Behold the sparrow findeth
   A house in which to rest,
The swallow has discovered
   Where she may build her nest;
And where, securely sheltered,
   Her young she forth may bring;
So LORD of hosts, Thy altars
   I seek, my God, my King.

4 Blest who Thy house inhabit,
   They ever give Thee praise;
5 Blest all whom Thou dost
   strengthen,
Who love the sacred ways.
6 Who pass through Baca's valley,
   And make in it a well;
There rains in shower abundant
   The pools with water fill.

72

7 So they from strength unwearied
Go forward unto strength,
Till they appear in Zion,
Before the Lord at length.
8 O hear, LORD God of Jacob,
To me an answer yield;
9 The face of Thy Anointed,
Behold, O God, our Shield.

10 One day excels a thousand,
If spent Thy courts within;
I'll choose a threshold rather
Than dwell in tents of sin.
11 Our sun and shield Jehovah,
Will grace and glory give;
No good will He deny them
That uprightly do live.

12 O God of hosts, Jehovah,
How blest is every one
Who confidence reposes
On Thee, O LORD, alone.
1 O LORD of hosts, how lovely
The place where thou dost dwell.
Thy tabernacles holy
In pleasantness excel.

TUNE: LLANGLOFFAN 76.76.D (31F)
("O Lord of Hosts, How Lovely")

Book of Psalms, 1871

Psalm 85

1 LORD, thine heart in love hath
yearned
On Thy lost and fallen land;
Isr'el's race is homeward turned,
2 Thou hast freed Thy captive band:
Thou hast borne Thy people's sin,
Covered all their deeds of ill;
3 All Thy wrath is gathered in,
And Thy burning anger still.

4 Turn us, stay us, now once more,
God of all our health and peace;
Let Thy cloud of wrath flee o'er,
From Thine own thy fury cease.
5 Wilt Thou ne'er the storm assuage
On the realm of thy desire,

Length'ning out from age to age
Thy consuming jealous ire?

6 Wilt Thou not in mercy turn?
Turn, and be our life again,
That Thy people's heart may burn
With the gladness of Thy reign.
7 Show us now Thy tender love;
Thy salvation, LORD, impart;
8 I the voice divine would prove,
List'ning in my silent heart:

List'ning what the LORD will say
"Peace" to all that own His will:
To his saints that love His way,
"Peace," and "turn no more to ill."
9 Ye that fear Him, nigh at hand
Now His saving health ye find,
That the glory in our land,
As of old, may dwell enshrined.

10 Mercy now and justice meet,
Peace and truth for aye embrace;
11 Truth from earth is
springing sweet,
Justice looks from her high place.
12 Nor will GOD his goodness stay,
Nor our land her bounteous store:
13 Marking out her Maker's way,
Righteousness shall go before.

TUNE:ST. GEORGE'S WINDSOR 77.77.
("Come, Ye Thankful People, Come")
(new *Trinity Hymnal,* p. 715)
or ST. BEES 77.77.
new *Trinity Hymnal,* p. 586)
("Hark My Soul")

Irish Psalter, 1880

Psalm 86

Verses 1–11

1 Bow down Thy ear, O Lord,
       and hear,
    For I am poor and great my need;
2 Preserve my soul, for Thee I fear;
    O God, Thy trusting servant heed.
3 O Lord, be merciful to me,
    For all the day to Thee I cry;
4 Rejoice Thy servant, for to Thee
    I lift my soul, O Lord Most High.

5 For Thou, O Lord, art good
       and kind,
    And ready to forgive Thou art;
    Abundant mercy they shall find
    Who call on Thee with all
       their heart.
6 O Lord, incline Thy ear to me,
    My voice of supplication heed;
7 In trouble I will cry to Thee,
    For Thou wilt answer when
       I plead.

8 There is no God but Thee alone,
    Nor works like Thine, O Lord
       Most High;
9 All nations, Lord, shall round
       Thy throne
    Their great Creator glorify.
10 In all Thy deeds how great
       Thou art!
    Thou one true God, Thy way
       make clear;
11 Teach me, O Lord, unite my heart
    To trust Thy truth, Thy Name
       to fear.

Verses 12–17

12 O Lord, my God, my joyful heart
    Will give Thee praise
       for evermore,
13 For rich in grace to me Thou art,
    My soul from death Thou
       didst restore.

14 O God, the proud against me rise,
    The wicked who delight in strife;
    They set not Thee before
       their eyes,
    They seek to take away my life.

15 But, Lord, in Thee all grace
       is found,
    Thou God Who dost compassion
       show.
    Thy truth and goodness
       still abound,
    To wrath and anger Thou
       art slow.

16 In mercy turn and look on me,
    Thy servant true, Thy chosen one;
    Let me Thy great salvation see,
    And strengthen me my course
       to run.

17 Some token of Thy love bestow,
    Which they who hate me now
       may see;
    Let all, O Lord, be brought
       to know
    That Thou dost help and
       comfort me.

TUNE: LLEF LM
(new *Trinity Hymnal*, 91)

The Psalter, 1912; altered 1994

Psalm 87

1 Upon the holy hills the Lord
Has His foundation laid;
2 He loves the gates of Zion more
Than dwellings Jacob made.

3 O city of our God, there are
Things glorious said of thee.
4 I'll mention Egypt, Babylon,
Among those knowing me.

Include the land of Palestine;
Let Tyre the survey share,
With distant Ethiopia:
"This is a man born there!"

5 And so of Zion it is said,
"Each one was born in her;"
And He that is Himself Most High,
He has established her.

6 The Lord, when listing peoples,
notes,
"This is a man born there!"
7 And singers with their
minstrels say,
"Our fountains in thee are."

TUNE: RICHMOND CM
(new *Trinity Hymnal*, p. 83)
("City of God")
("O Praise the Lord, for He Is Good")

Psalm 88

Verses 1–8

1 O Lord, the God of my
salvation tried,
All day and night before Thee
I have cried.
2 O let my prayer before
Thy presence rise;
Incline Thine ear to hear
my pleading cries.

3 My soul is full of anxious cares
and gloom;
My weary life draws nigh
the silent tomb.
4 I count as those that to the
pit descend;
I'm like the man whose strength
is at an end.

5 As one cast off among the
dead am I;
I'm like the pierced ones in
the grave that lie,
Whom Thou hast not remembered
any more,
Those cut off from Thy hand
where none restore.

6 By Thee within the lowest pit
I'm laid,
In deeps and in the place
of darkest shade;
7 Thy furious wrath on me
has come to rest,
And with Thy breakers Thou
hast me oppressed.

8 My former friends Thou hast
estranged from me;
Yes, their abhorrence I am made
by Thee;
Shut up am I, imprisoned
here must stay;
Through deep distress my eyes
both waste away.

(Turn page for next section)

9 O LORD, I've daily called upon
  Thy name,
   Spread forth my hands Thy
   gracious help to claim.
10 Wilt Thou Thy wonders make the
  dead to know?
   And shall the dead arise Thy
   praise to show?

11 Shall Thy great love be in the
  grave extolled?
   Or shall Thy truth be in
   destruction told?
12 In darkness who Thy wonders
  will confess,
   Where mem'ries fade make
   known Thy righteousness?

13 But unto Thee, Jehovah,
   I have cried;
   My prayer shall rise to Thee with
   morningtide.
14 O LORD, why dost Thou cast my
  soul from Thee?
   Why dost Thou hide Thy gracious
   face from me?

15 From youth I am distressed,
   about to die;
   Thy terrors I have borne;
   distraught was I.
16 Thy burning anger over me
   has passed;
   Thy terrors all have
   cut me off at last.

17 All day like billows they around
  me surge;
   Together closing in they me
   submerge.
18 Thou hast put far from me each
   lover, friend,
   And my acquaintances in darkness
   end.

TUNE: ELLERS 10.10.10.10. (88B)
("Savior Again, to Thy Dear Name")

Psalm 89

Verses 1–16

1 Of GOD's love I'll sing forever,
   To each age Your faithfulness.
2 I'll declare Your love's forever,
   Founded in the word from heav'n:
3 "With My Chosen I've made
   cov'nant,
   To My servant David sworn:
4 'I'll your line confirm forever,
   To each age build up your
   throne.'"

5 LORD, the heavens praise Your
   wonders,
   Angels sing your faithfulness.
6 For none matches GOD in heaven,
   Who's like GOD in heaven's
   throng?
7 God is feared among the angels,
   He's more awesome than they all.
8 LORD, O God of hosts,
   who's like You?
   Mighty God, You're girt with truth.

9 You rule over sea's proud surging;
   When its waves rise,
   bid them still.
10 You broke Egypt, left her dying;
   Your strong arm dispersed
   Your foes.
11 Yours the heavens,
   earth's bounds also;
   You have founded all the world.
12 North and south You
   have created;
   Tabor, Hermon, praise Your name.

13 You've an arm that's great
   in pow-er;
   Your strong hand is all supreme.
14 Your rule's based on right
   and justice;
   Cov'nant love and truth are yours.
15 They are happy who acclaim you;
   In Your favour, LORD, they walk.
16 In Your name rejoicing ever;
   In Your righteousness raised high.

17 Lord, our boast is in Your power;
   You exalt us in Your love.
18 For our king is GOD's, and Is-r'el's
   Holy One our sovereign owns.
19 You revealed Your word in vision
   To Your faithful ones of old:
   "I've giv'n pow-er to a strong one;
   Raised one chosen from My folk.

20 "I have found my servant David;
   With My oil anointed him.
21 My hand will be ever with him,
   And My pow'r will make
      him strong.
22 None to tribute will subject him,
   Nor will wicked ones oppress.
23 I will crush his foes before him;
   Those who hate him I'll
      strike down.

24 "My strong love and truth is with
      him;
   I will raise his head up high;
25 To the Sea his rule extending,
   And to rivers in the east.
26 He will cry: 'You are my Father;
   You're my God, my saviour, rock.'
27 I'll appoint him as My firstborn,
   Highest of the kings of earth.

28 "I'll keep love for him forever,
   My oath to him will not fail.
29 I'll his line establish always,
   And his throne for evermore.
30 If his sons forsake My teaching,
31 Break My laws, commands
      and rules,
32 I'll their sins severely punish,
33 But not take my love from him.

   "I'll maintain My faithful promise.
34 I'll not break my covenant,
   Nor take back the words
      I've uttered.
35 This I've pledged in holiness;
   And I'll not be false to David.
36 Like the sun his line will last;
37 Like the moon his throne
      before Me;
   Heaven's witness faithful stands."

38 Yet You have cut off, rejected;
   Your Anointed knows Your wrath.
39 You've defiled Your servant's
      cov'nant,
   You have thrown his crown
      to earth.
40 You have broken down his fences,
   Brought his strongholds to
      the ground.
41 All who pass by have him
      plundered.
   He's the jest of nations near.

42 You his foes have raised in pow-er,
   Made his enemies rejoice.
43 You have made his sword turn
      backwards,
   You've not strengthened him
      to fight.
44 You've deprived him of his glory,
   Cast his throne down to the ground.
45 Old before his time You've
      made him,
   You have covered him with shame.

46 How long, LORD? Will You
      hide always?
   Your wrath ever burn like fire?
47 O recall how short my life is;
   Have You made all men for naught?
48 Who alive is free from dying
   Who the grave's power will escape?
49 Lord, where is Your
      cov'nant promise
   You to David swore in truth?

50 Lord, remember all the insults
   Which Your servants bear for You.
   In my heart I bear the insults
   Taunting nations cast on them.
51 Insults, LORD, for Your Anointed,
   Mocking ev'ry step he takes.
52 Yet, LORD, You are ever blessed,
   So I say, Amen! Amen!

TUNE: ODE TO JOY 87.87.D
(new *Trinity Hymnal*, p. 122)
("God, All Nature Sings Thy Glory")
*The Complete Book of Psalms for
Singing, 1991; altered 1994*

Psalm 90

Verses 1–9

1 Lord, Thou hast been our
 dwelling place
 Through all the ages of our race.
2 Before the mountains had
 their birth,
 Or ever Thou hadst formed
 the earth,
 From years which no
 beginning had
 To years unending, Thou art God.

3 Thou turnest man to dust again,
 And say'st, "Return, ye sons
 of men."
4 As yesterday when past appears,
 So are to Thee a thousand years;
 They like a day are in Thy sight,
 Yes, like a passing watch
 by night.

5 Thou with a flood hast
 swept men on;
 They like a sleep are
 quickly gone.
 They are like grass which
 grows each morn;
6 Its blades of green the
 fields adorn.
 At morn its sprouts and
 blossoms rise;
 At eve, cut down, it withered lies.

7 For by Thine anger we're
 consumed,
 And by Thy wrath to
 terror doomed.
8 Our sins Thou in Thy sight
 dost place,
 Our secret faults before Thy face;
9 So in Thy wrath our days we end,
 And like a sigh our years
 we spend.

Verses 10–17

10 For some life's years are seventy;
 Perhaps the strong may
 eighty see;
 Their best involves but toil
 and woe;
 All quickly ends. How soon
 we go!
11 Who has Thine anger understood?
 Who fears Thy fury as he should?

12 O teach Thou us to count
 our days
 And set our hearts on
 wisdom's ways.
13 How long, O LORD? Return!
 Repent,
 And toward Thy servants
 now relent.
14 Each morning fill us with
 Thy grace;
 We'll sing for joy through
 all our days.

15 According to the days we spent
 Beneath affliction Thou hast sent,
 And all the years we evil knew,
 Now make us glad,
 our joy renew.
16 Thy work in all Thy
 servants show;
 Thy glory on their sons bestow.

17 On us let there be shed abroad
 The beauty of the LORD our God.
 Our handiwork upon us be
 Established evermore by Thee.
 Yes, let our handiwork now be
 Established evermore by Thee.

TUNE: ST. CATHERINE 88.88.88. (90C)
("Faith of Our Fathers")
Based on *The Book of Psalms,* 1871, and
The Psalter, 1912

Psalm 91

1 Who with God Most High
    finds shelter
In th'Almighty's shadow hides.
2 To the LORD I'll say, "My Refuge!"
In my God my trust abides.
3 From the fowler's snare
    He'll save you,
From the deadly pestilence;
4 Cover you with outspread pinions,
Make His wings your confidence.

God's own truth, your shield
    and buckler;
5 You will fear no ill by night,
Nor the shafts in daylight flying,
6 Nor disease that shuns the light,
Nor the plague that wastes
    at noonday.
7 At your side ten thousand fall;
8 You will only see this judgment
Which rewards the wicked all.

9 You have made the LORD
    your refuge,
God Most High your
    dwelling-place;
10 Nothing evil shall befall you;
In your tent no scourge
    you'll face.
11 He will angels charge to
    keep you,
Guard you well in all your ways.
12 In their hands they will
    uphold you
Lest your foot a stone
    should graze.

13 You shall trample serpents, lions,
Tread on all your deadly foes.
14 For his love to Me I'll save him,
Keep him, for My name
    he knows;
15 When he calls Me I will answer,
Save and honor him will I.
16 I will show him my salvation,
With long life will satisfy.

TUNE: HYFRYDOL 87.87.D (91A)
("Jesus What a Friend for Sinners")

Psalm 92

1 It's good to thank the LORD,
To praise Your name, Most High!
2 To show Your love at dawn,
Your faithfulness all night!
3 The ten-stringed lyre
With sweet-voiced lute and
    rippling harp
Your praise inspire.

4 Your deeds, LORD, made me glad.
I'll joy in what You've done.
5 How great Your doings, LORD!
How deep Your thoughts
    each one!
6 Fools won't be shown;
The foolish can't accept this truth,
To him unknown!

7 Though sinners grow like weeds,
Ill-do-ers blossom may,
8 They're doomed to be destroyed.
You, LORD, exalted stay.
9 LORD, Your foes fall.
See! How Your foes, vain
    evil men,
Are scattered all!

10 You've raised, like ox, my horn,
Poured fresh oil on my head.
11 You made me see the spies
And hear what plotters said.
12 Like thriving palm
The righteous grows, like
    cedars tall
On Lebanon.

13 Those planted by the LORD
Shall in God's courts be seen;
14 When old they'll still bear fruit
And flourish fresh and green,
15 And loud proclaim
How upright is the LORD,
    my Rock;
No wrong in Him!

TUNE: DARWALL'S 148th 66.66.4444.
(92C)
("Rejoice the Lord Is King")
("Join All the Glorious Names")

Psalm 93

1 Jehovah reigns; He's clothed
With majesty most bright;
Jehovah is arrayed with strength;
He girds Himself with might.

Established is the world,
Its steadfast place to hold.
2 And Thou from everlasting art;
Thy throne is fixed of old.

3 The floods, O LORD, lift up,
The floods lift up their voice.
The floods are lifting up
their waves;
They make a mighty noise.

4 But yet the LORD on high
More mighty far is He
Than is the thunder of the waves
Or breakers of the sea.

5 Thy testimonies all
In faithfulness excel;
And holiness, forever, LORD,
Thine house becometh well.

TUNE: ST. MICHAEL/OLD 134TH SM
(new *Trinity Hymnal,* p. 78) or
RIALTO SM (93A)

Based on the *Book of Psalms,* 1871

Psalm 94

1 God of vengeance, O Jehovah,
God of vengeance, O shine forth!
2 Rise up, O You Judge of Nations!
Render to the proud their worth.
3 O LORD, how long shall
the wicked,
How long shall the wicked boast?
4 Arrogant the words they pour out,
Ill men all, a taunting host.

5 They, Jehovah, crush Your people
And Your heritage distress;
6 They kill sojourner and widow,
Murder they the fatherless.
7 And they say, "Jehovah sees not;
Jacob's God does not have eyes."
8 Understand, O foolish people!
When, O fools, will you be wise?

9 Who the ear made,
does He hear not?
Who formed eyes,
does He not see?
10 Who warns nations,
does He smite not?
Who men teaches, knows not He?
11 All the thoughts of men
the LORD sees,
Knows that but a breath are they.
12 Bless'd the man whom You
chastise, LORD,
Whom You teach to know
Your Way.

13 Give him rest from days
of trouble,
Till the wicked be o'erthrown.
14 Our LORD will not leave
His people,
Will abandon not His own.
15 When to every verdict given
Justice shall come back again,
Everyone whose heart is upright
Will see righteous judgment then.

16 Who for me withstands
the wicked?
Who against wrong pleads for me?

17 If the LORD were not my helper,
   Soon my soul would silent be.
18 If I say, "My foot is slipping!"
   LORD, Your mercy will uphold.
19 When my anxious thoughts
      are many,
   How Your comforts cheer
      my soul!

20 Can destructive rulers join You
   And by law disorder build?
21 They conspire against
      the righteous,
   Sentence just ones to be killed.
22 But the LORD is still my
      stronghold;
   God, my Refuge, will repay.
23 He'll for sin wipe out the wicked;
   Them the LORD our God will slay.

TUNE: AUSTRIAN HYMN 87.87.D. (94A)
("Glorious Things of Thee Are Spoken")

Psalm 95

Verses 1–5

1 O come and to Jehovah sing;
   Let us our voices raise;
   In joyful songs let us the Rock
   Of our salvation praise.
2 Before His presence let us come
   With praise and thankful voice;
   Let us sing psalms to Him
      with grace;
   With shouts let us rejoice.

3 The LORD's a mighty God
      and King;
   Above all gods He is.
4 The depths of earth are in
      His hand;
   The mountain peaks are His.
5 To Him the spacious sea belongs;
   'Twas made by His command;
   And by the working of His hands
   He formed the rising land.

Verses 6–11

6 O come and let us worship Him;
   Let us with one accord
   In presence of our Maker kneel,
   And bow before the LORD.
7 Because He only is our God,
   And we His chosen sheep,
   The people of His pasturage,
   Whom His own hand will keep.

   Today if you will hear His voice,
8 Then harden not your heart;
   Strive not as those at Meribah,
   Nor Massah's testing start.
9 Your fathers tried and
      tempted Me,
   Though they My work perceived;
10 And with that generation I
   For forty years was grieved.

   I said, "They have a
      wand'ring heart,
   And they My ways detest."
11 In wrath I swore they should
      not come
   Into My promised rest.

TUNE: IRISH CM (83B)

Based on the *Book of Psalms*, 1871 and
The Psalter, 1912

81

Psalm 96

1 O sing a new song to the Lord;
   All earth sing to the Lord.
2 Sing to the Lord, and bless His name;
   "He saves!" each day proclaim.
3 His glory to all nations show;
   His deeds let peoples know.

4 The Lord is great. How great
      His praise!
   Above all gods He's feared.
5 For heathen gods are idols vain;
   The Lord the heavens made.
6 Before Him honor, majesty,
   And strength and splendor be!

7 O families of earth, ascribe
   All glory to the Lord!
   All strength ascribe unto the Lord;
8 The glory of His name
   Give to the Lord. To His courts come
   And bring an offering.

9 In beautiful and holy robes
   Bring worship to the Lord.
   All earth, before Him stand in awe;
10 Proclaim, "The Lord is King!"
   Controlled by Him, the world
      stands firm;
   His judgments justice bless.

11 Let heav'ns be glad and earth rejoice.
   In vast expanse untold
   Let seas speak out with endless roar.
12 Let fields and all they hold
   Their glory give; let trees and
      woods
   With rustling boughs give praise.

13 Let all prepare to greet the Lord,
   Because he coming is.
   He surely comes to judge the earth.
   And righteousness is His.
   He'll nations judge with faithfulness,
   The world with justice bless.

TUNE: CORONATION 86.86.86. (96A)
("All Hail the Power")

Elements from the *Book of Psalms*, 1871
and *The Psalter*, 1912

Psalm 97

1 Jehovah reigns; let earth be glad;
   Let isles their joy make known;
2 Dark clouds surround Him,
      and on right
   And justice rests His throne.
3 Fire goes before Him,
      and His foes
   It burns up round about;
4 His lightnings lightened all
      the world;
   Earth saw and shook throughout.

5 Before the Lord the
      mountains melt
   As wax before a flame,
   Before the Lord of all the earth
   As near His presence came.
6 The heav'ns declare His
      righteousness;
   All men His glory see.
7 All serving graven images
   Confused and shamed shall be.

   They who of idols boast
      are shamed;
   To Him gods worship bring.
8 When Zion hears this, she is glad,
   And Judah's daughters sing,
   Because of all Thy judgments,
      Lord.
9 Thou art the Lord Most High
   Above all earth, above all gods
   Exalted very high.

10 Hate evil, all who love the Lord;
   He keeps His saints secure,
   And from the hand of
      wicked men
   He gives deliv'rance sure.
11 For all the righteous light is sown,
   And true hearts gladness claim.
12 Ye righteous, in the Lord rejoice,
   And thank His holy name.

TUNE: ST. ANNE CM (37A)
("O God Our Help in Ages Past")

Based on *Scottish Psalter*, 1650

Psalm 98

1 O sing a new song to the LORD
For wonders He has done,
His right hand and His holy arm
The victory have won.

2 The great salvation wrought
by Him
Jehovah has made known.
His justice in the nations' sight
The Lord has clearly shown.

3 He mindful of His grace and truth
To Isr'el's house has been.
The great salvation of our God
All ends of earth have seen.

4 O all the earth, sing to the LORD
And make a joyful sound.
Lift up your voice aloud to Him;
Sing psalms! Let joy resound!

5 With harp make music to
the LORD;
With harp a psalm O sing!
6 With horn and trumpet raise
a shout
Before the LORD, the King.

7 Let seas in all their vastness roar,
The world, its living horde.
8 Let rivers clap, let mountains sing
Their joy before the LORD!

9 Because He comes,
He surely comes
The judge of earth to be!
With justice he will judge
the world
All men with equity.

TUNE: DESERT CM (98A) or
ANTIOCH CM

Based on *Scottish Psalter*, 1650

Psalm 99

1 The LORD is King indeed!
Let peoples quail and fear!
He sits above the cherubim;
Let earth be moved!
2 The LORD in Zion rules,
And over all is high;
3 O praise His great and
dreadful name,
The Holy One!

4 The pow-er of the King
Delights in equity;
In Jacob You establish law
And righteousness.
5 Exalt and celebrate
The LORD, Who is our God,
And at His footstool worship Him,
The Holy One!

6 For Moses was His priest,
And Aaron, too, did serve,
And Samuel of them who called
Upon His name.
The LORD received their cry;
7 He spoke from out the cloud.
His testimonies they obeyed;
They kept His laws.

8 O LORD our God, You heard,
And answer gave to them;
You were a God that bore
them up
But judged their works!
9 Exalt the LORD our God!
Bow to His holy hill!
Behold, He is the Holy One,
The LORD our God!

TUNE: LEONI 6.6.8.4.D (99C)
("The God of Abraham Praise")

Psalm 100

1 All people that on earth do dwell,
Sing to the LORD with
cheerful voice.
2 Him serve with mirth; His praise
forth tell;
Come ye before Him and rejoice.

3 Know that the LORD is
God indeed;
Without our aid He did us make.
We are His folk; He doth us feed,
And for His sheep He doth
us take.

4 O enter then His gates
with praise;
Within His courts your thanks
proclaim;
With grateful hearts your
voices raise
To bless and magnify His name.

5 Because the LORD our God
is good,
His mercy is forever sure;
His truth at all times firmly stood
And shall from age to age endure.

TUNE: OLD 100TH LM (100A)

Based on William Kethe and
Scottish Psalter, 1564

Psalm 101

1 Of mercy and of justice,
O LORD, I'll sing to Thee.
2 In uprightness and wisdom
Shall my behavior be.
O when in lovingkindness
Wilt Thou to me come near?
I'll walk within my dwelling
With heart and life sincere.

3 I will permit no base thing
Before my eyes to be.
I hate unfaithful doing;
It shall not cleave to me.
4 The man whose heart is froward
Shall from my presence go;
And nothing that is evil
Will I consent to know.

5 I'll cut him off that slanders
His neighbor secretly;
I'll not endure the proud heart
Nor eyes that haughty be.
6 My eyes are with the faithful
That he may dwell with me;
The man whose walk is upright
My minister shall be.

7 No man of works deceitful
Within my house shall dwell;
Nor in my sight shall tarry
A man who lies will tell.
8 Each morning with destruction
The wicked I'll reward,
To free from evildoers
The city of the LORD.

TUNE: AURELIA 76.76.D (101)
("The Church's One Foundation")

Based on the *Book of Psalms*, 1871

84

Psalm 102

Verses 1–12

1 To this my prayer O listen, LORD!
And let my cry for help reach You.
2 In day of grief hide not Your face.
Your list'ning ear toward me
O bend;
The day I call, Your answer send.

3 For all my days go up in smoke,
And like a hearth my bones
are burned.
4 Like grass my heart is crushed
and dried;
I daily food forgotten leave;
5 My skin and bones together
cleave.

With sighs and groans my
frame resounds.
6 I'm like a desert pelican,
Or like an owl in ruined wastes.
7 I lie awake, as on the roof
A sparrow stands, alone, aloof.

8 All day my foes their taunts
repeat;
Those filled with anger curse
my name.
9 I food with tears and ashes mix,
10 For You on me in anger frown;
You raised me up to throw
me down.

11 An ev'ning shadow are my days;
Like grass I wither soon away.
12 But You, Jehovah, sit enthroned
Forever; Your memorial
Abides through generations all.

Verses 13–22

13 Arise! On Zion mercy have!
The time to favor her has come.
14 Your servants love her dust
and stones.
15 So Gentiles will the LORD's name
fear,
Your glory kings of earth revere.

16 The LORD in glory has appeared,
17 Has rebuilt Zion, heard her prayer,
18 The destitute has not despised.
This work shall ages all record
That men unborn may
praise the LORD.

19 He from His holy height
looked down;
The LORD from heaven viewed
the earth,
20 To hear the groans of prisoners
And free those who were
doomed to die,
21 That men the LORD may magnify.

In Zion let all men declare
The glory of Jehovah's name,
His praise tell in Jerusalem,
22 When peoples all with one accord,
Assembling, worship there
the LORD.

Verses 23–28

23 My strength He weakened
in the way;
24 My days He shortened. Then I pled,
"In mid-life take me not away,
O God, Whose years will
never end,
But will through ages all extend."

25 Of old You earth's foundation laid;
Your mighty hands the
heavens made;
26 Yet they will die, while You endure.
Like garments they will worn out be;
Like clothes You change them
constantly.

These shall be changed and
pass away;
27 But You are evermore the same,
Because Your years will never end.
28 Your servants' children dwell secure
Before You, reestablished sure.

TUNE: PARK STREET LM (102B)

vv. 13-22 altered 1994

85

Psalm 103

Verses 1–13

1 Bless the Lord, my soul;
   my whole heart
2 Ever bless His holy name.
   Bless the Lord, my soul; forget not
   All His mercies to proclaim.
3 Who forgives all thy
   transgressions,
   Thy diseases all Who heals;
4 Who redeems thee from
   destruction,
   Who with thee so kindly deals.

   Who with love and mercy
   crowns thee,
5 Satisfies thy mouth with good,
   So that even like the eagle
   Thou art blessed with
   youth renewed.
6 In His righteousness Jehovah
   Will deliver those distressed;
   He will execute just judgment
   In the cause of all oppressed.

7 He made known His ways
   to Moses,
   And His acts to Isr'el's race;
8 Tender, loving is Jehovah
   Slow to anger, rich in grace.
9 He will not forever chide us
   Nor will keep His anger still,
10 Has not dealt as we offended
   Nor requited us our ill.

11 For as high as is the heaven,
   Far above the earth below,
   Ever great to them that fear Him
   Is the mercy He will show.
12 Far as east from west is distant
   He has put away our sin;
13 Like the pity of a father
   Has Jehovah's pity been.

Verses 14–22

14 For our frame He well remembers;
   That we are but dust He knows;
15 As for man, like grass he rises;

As the flower in field he grows;
16 Over it the wind now passes;
   In a moment it is gone;
   In the place where once it
   flourished
   It shall never more be known.

17 But Jehovah's loving kindness
   Unto them that fear His name
   From eternity abideth
   To eternity the same.
   And His righteousness remaineth
   To their children and their seed,
18 Who His covenant remember
   And His precepts hear and heed.

19 In the heavens has Jehovah
   Founded His eternal throne;
   Over all is His dominion;
   He is king and He alone.
20 Bless the Lord, all you His angels,
   You on whom He strength
   conferred,
   Who His orders are performing,
   Who obey His every word.

21 Bless the Lord, all you
   His servants,
   Hosts that know and do His will,
   Who forever wait upon Him,
   All His pleasure to fulfill.
22 Bless the Lord,
   all you His creatures,
   All His works with one accord
   In all parts of His dominion.
   O my soul, bless thou the Lord.

TUNE: BEECHER 87.87.D (103A)
("Love Divine All Loves Excelling")

Based on the *Book of Psalms*, 1871 and
The Psalter, 1912; vv. 20-22 altered 1994

Psalm 104

Verses 1–12

1 My soul, bless the Lord!
      Lord God, You are great!
   With honor arrayed,
      majestic in state,
2 You cover Yourself with a
      garment of light
   And stretch out the sky as a
      curtain by night.

3 The beams of Your courts
      in waters You laid;
   On wings of the wind
      Your pathway You made.
4 The clouds are Your chariot;
      the winds do Your will;
   The flames and the lightnings
      Your pleasure fulfill.

5 You set up the earth
      on foundations sure,
   That always it should
      unshaken endure.
6 The deep like a garment about
      it You cast;
   The waters stood high; over
      mountains they passed.

7 But at Your rebuke the
      high waters fled;
   Your thunder they heard
      and fast away sped.
8 The mountains arose, and the
      valleys sank low;
   The place You appointed for
      them now they know.

9 To hold waters fast
      You set up their bound,
   Lest turning again
      they cover the ground.
10 You make springs gush forth
      in the valleys below
   And cause rushing streams
      between mountains to flow.

11 The beast of the field
      they furnish with drink;

The wild asses quench their thirst
      on the brink.
12 The birds make their nests in the
      trees by the spring;
   And there in the branches they
      joyfully sing.

Verses 13–23

13 You water the hills
      with rain from Your sky,
   With fruit of Your works
      the earth satisfy.
14 To nourish the cattle You cause
      grass to grow;
   For creatures who serve man the
      plants You bestow.

So man brings forth food
      by working the earth;
15 And wine that he grows
      his heart fills with mirth;
   To make his face shine he
      extracts fragrant oil
   And finds bread that strengthens
      his heart for his toil.

16 The trees of the Lord
      are all watered well;
   Great cedars high up
      on Lebanon dwell.
17 There birds build their nests;
      the stork makes firs its home.
18 On high rocks the badgers and
      goats safely roam.

19 The moon You have set
      the seasons to show;
   The sun will its time
      for each setting know.
20 When You make the darkness,
      the night follows day,
   And beasts of the forest
      creep forth seeking prey.

21 The young lions roar,
      from God begging meat,
22 But at the sunrise
      they quickly retreat,
   And deep in their dens
      all day hide from the light,
23 While man works and labors
      abroad till the night.
   (Turn page for next section)

24 How many works, LORD,
    in wisdom You've made!
  How full on the earth,
    Your riches displayed!
25 Out yonder the ocean,
    how great and how wide,
  Where small and great creatures
    unnumbered abide!

26 Where ships sail the deep,
    Leviathans play;
27 These all look to You
    to give food each day.
28 Whatever You give them
    they gather for food;
  When Your hand You open
    You fill them with good.

29 When You hide Your face,
    bewildered they yearn.
30 When You take their breath,
    to dust they return.
  When You send Your spirit,
    created are they.
  The face of the ground
    You renew every day.

31 Forever O may
    the LORD's glory stand!
  The LORD shall enjoy
    each work of His hand.
32 He looks on the earth
    and it trembles in fear;
  When He touches mountains,
    the smoke will appear.

33 I'll sing to the LORD
    as long as I live,
  Sing praise to my God
    while life He will give.
34 My thoughts about Him
    will sweet pleasure afford.
  For I am rejoicing
    each day in the LORD.

35 Consumed from the earth
    let sinners then be;
  The wicked in life
    no more let us see.

And now, O my soul,
    blessing give to the LORD.
Let glad hallelujahs ring;
    O praise the LORD!

TUNE: LYONS 10.10.11.11. (104A)
("O Worship the King")

Elements from *The Psalter,* 1912

Psalm 105

Verses 1–22

1 O thank the LORD;
    on His name call.
  His deeds tell peoples all.
2 O sing to Him,
    sing psalms to Him,
  His wonders all recall.
3 Let hearts that seek
    the LORD rejoice,
  His holy name adore.
4 O seek Jehovah and His strength,
  His face seek evermore.

5 Remember all His miracles,
  The judgments He has done,
6 O Abrah'ms children, serving Him
  All Jacob's sons, His own.
7 He only is the LORD our God;
  His judgments fill the land.
8 He keeps in mind His covenant
  That it may always stand.

  A thousand ages to endure
  Commanded He His word,
9 With Abrah'm made a covenant,
  The promise Isaac heard,
10 A law to Jacob He confirmed,
  A bond for Is-ra-el:
11 "I will to you give Canaan's land,
  Where you as heir may dwell."

12 When few in number,
    scarcely known,
  They sojourned in the land,
13 From nation on to nation went,
  A restless, wand'ring band,

88

14 He let none hurt them,
    for their sakes
To kings He gave alarm:
15 "Touch not My own
    anointed ones,
Nor do My prophets harm."

16 When He brought famine
    on the land
And broke their staff of bread,
17 The Joseph they sold as a slave
He had sent on ahead.
18 His feet they hurt with
    fetters strong
And him in irons did bind;
19 Till what he prophesied
    came true,
The LORD's word him refined.

20 The king, the peoples' ruler, sent
To loose and set him free;
21 He made him lord of
    all his house,
Guard of his wealth to be.
22 He gave him pow'r to bind at will
The princes of the land,
To share his wisdom, and to make
His elders understand.

Verses 23–45

23 When Is-ra-el to Egypt came,
When Jacob journeyed west
To settle in the land of Ham,
24 The LORD his children blessed.
He made them stronger than
    their foes,
25 Whose hearts He filled with hate
That made them hunt His
    people out,
His servants chide and cheat.

26 Then He His servant Moses sent
And Aaron whom He chose.
27 They miracles in Egypt wrought,
His signs among their foes.
28 He darkness sent, the land
    made dark,
So they His words might try.
29 He turned their waters into blood
And caused their fish to die.

30 He made their land to swarm
    with frogs,
Kings' chambers filled with them.
31 He spoke, and swarms of flies
    and gnats
Throughout their country came.
32 He gave them hail instead of rain,
Flashed lightning through
    their land;
33 He smote their fig trees and
    their vines,
Slashed trees on ev'ry hand.

34 He spoke, and countless
    locusts came,
35 Their fruits and leaves devoured.
36 He killed each firstborn
    in the land,
The princes of their power.
37 He led His people forth enriched
With silver and with gold,
And there was none
    among His tribes
Who stumbled, young or old.

38 How glad was Egypt
    when they went!
It shook with dread of them.
39 He spread a cloud to cover them;
By night it shined like flame.
40 At their request He brought
    them quails;
He bread from heav'n bestowed.
41 He split the rock and water gushed;
Through desert lands it flowed.

42 His holy promise He recalled,
How Abrah'm served Him long.
43 He led His people forth with joy,
His chosen ones with song.
44 The nations' lands, the
    peoples' toil,
He gave them for their own,
45 That they should keep and
    heed His law.
O praise the LORD alone.

TUNE: NOEL CMD (21A)
("O Lord, by Grace Delivered")

vv. 5–6 altered 1994

89

Psalm 106

Verses 1–12

1 O praise the LORD!
   O thank the LORD!
   For bountiful is He;
   Because His lovingkindness lasts
   To all eternity.
2 Who can express Jehovah's praise
   Or tell His deeds of might?
3 O blessed are they who
      justice keep
   And ever do the right.

4 Regard me with the favor, LORD,
   Which Thou dost bear to Thine.
   O visit Thou my soul in love;
   Make Thy salvation mine;
5 That I may see Thy people's good
   And in their joy rejoice,
   And may with Thine inheritance
   Exult with cheerful voice.

6 With all our fathers we
      have sinned,
   Iniquity have done;
   We have gone on in wickedness,
   In evil ways have run.
7 Our fathers did not understand
   Thy works in Egypt done;
   Of all Thy many mercies shown,
   They did remember none.

   Though at the sea,
      the Sea of Reeds,
   They were rebellious grown,
8 He saved them for His own
      name's sake,
   To make His pow-er known.
9 And so the Red Sea He rebuked;
   It dried at His command.
   And then He led them through
      the depths
   As through the desert land.

10 And from the hand that
      hated them,
   He did His people save,

And from the hand of enemies
To them redemption gave.
11 The water overwhelmed
      their foes;
   None lived of all their throng.
12 His people then believed
      His words
   And praised His name in song.

Verses 13–31

13 The people soon forgot
      His works,
   Nor waited for His will;
14 They lusted in the wilderness,
   And God they tempted still.
15 He filled them with the meat
      they craved,
   A plague made their reward.
16 Men envied Moses,
      Aaron scorned,
   One holy to the LORD.

17 The op'ning earth on
      Dathan closed,
   Abiram's band entombed;
18 A fire blazed in their company
   And wicked ones consumed.
19 Yet they at Horeb made a calf,
   Before an image kneeled;
20 They made their glory like an ox
   That eats grass in the field.

21 Then God their Savior they forgot,
   Great things in Egypt done,
22 In Ham's land, by the Sea
      of Reeds,
   His awesome deeds each one.
23 He said He'd cut them off, unless
   Before Him in the way
   He'd chosen Moses there to stand
   And turn His wrath away.

24 Then they despised the
      pleasant land,
   Did not believe His word,
25 But, grumbling in their tents,
      refused
   To hearken to the LORD.

He therefore swore to cast
    them down
26 There in the desert sands,
    Among the nations cast their seed,
27 And scatter through the lands.

28 To Baal-Peor they were joined,
    Ate off'rings to the dead,
29 Provoked His anger with
    their deeds;
    The plague among them spread.
30 Then Phin'has stood and
    interposed,
    And so the plague was stayed;
31 Forever this as righteousness
    To His account was paid.

Verses 32–48

32 At Meribah they angered Him,
    On Moses evil brought,
33 For they provoked his temper so
    His speech was rash and hot.
34 They would not heed the
    LORD's command
    The heathen tribes to slay,
35 But mingled with the nations all
    And learned their evil way.

36 When they the heathen
    idols served,
    These were to them a snare,
37 For they to demons sacrificed
    Their sons and daughters there.
38 They poured out guiltless blood,
    the blood
    Their sons and daughters shed
    When they, to idols sacrificed,
    On Canaan's altars bled.

Polluted was the land with blood,
39 And thus defiled were they
    In all their works; and with
    their acts
    They went the harlot's way.
40 Against the people kindled was
    The anger of the LORD;
    They so provoked His wrath
    that He
    His heritage abhorred.

41 He gave them to the nations'
    pow'r,
    Put haters in command;
42 Their foes oppressed them,
    and they were
    Subdued beneath their hand.
43 He many times delivered them,
    But rebels still were they
    In all their plans; so down
    they went
    In sin to pine away.

44 Yet their distress He looked upon
    When he had heard their cry,
45 And He remembered for
    their sake
    His covenant on high.
    Then He relented in His grace
    And for His mercies' sake;
46 He gave them pity from all those
    Who did them captive take.

47 Save us, O LORD,
    our gracious God,
    From heathen lands reclaim,
    That we may glory in Thy praise
    And thank Thy holy name.
48 Blessed be Jehovah, Isr'el's God,
    To all eternity.
    Let all the people say, "Amen."
    Praise to the LORD give ye.

TUNE: LEVEQUE CMD (106E)

vv. 15–16 altered 1994

Psalm 107

Verses 1–16

1 O praise the LORD, for He is good;
   His mercies still endure;
2 Thus say the ransomed
   of the LORD,
   From all their foes secure.
3 He gathered them from
   out the lands,
   From north, south, east, and west.
4 They wandered in the wilderness,
   No city found to rest.

5 Their weary soul within
   them faints
   When thirst and hunger press;
6 In trouble to the LORD they cried;
   He saved them from distress.
7 He made the way before
   them straight,
   And He became their guide,
   That they might to a city go
   In which they would abide.

8 Let them give thanks unto
   the LORD
   For all His kindness shown,
   And for His works so wonderful
   Which He to men makes known.
9 Because the longing soul by Him
   With food is satisfied;
   The hungry soul that looks to Him
   With goodness is supplied.

10 Some people in the
    darkness lived,
    In death's shade did abide,
    The prisoners of misery
    With chains of iron tied,
11 Because against the words of God
    They in rebellion turned,
    And counsel of the One
    Most High
    They had despised and spurned.

12 He therefore humbled them
    with toil;
    They fell without redress.

13 In trouble to the LORD they cried;
    He saved them from distress.
14 He brought them out
    of darkness great
    And took them from
    death's shade;
    He broke apart the iron bands
    Which had them helpless made.

15 Let them give thanks
    unto the LORD
    For all His kindness shown,
    And for His works so wonderful
    Which He to men makes known.
16 For He the mighty gates of bronze
    Has shattered with a stroke;
    He cut the bars of iron off
    And them asunder broke.

Verses 17–32

17 For trespass and iniquity
    Fools were afflicted here.
18 Their soul abhorred all food;
    and they
    To gates of death drew near.
19 In trouble to the LORD they cried;
    He saved them from distress;
20 He sent His word to make
    them whole
    And lift from wretchedness.

21 Let them give thanks
    unto the LORD
    For all His kindness shown,
    And for His works so wonderful
    Which He to men makes known.
22 And let them offer thanks to Him,
    The sacrifice of praise;
    His works let them
    declare abroad,
    In songs their voices raise.

23 To those who go to sea in ships
    And on great waters trade,
24 The works and wonders
    of the LORD
    Are in the deep displayed.
25 For His command stirred
    up the wind

That with a tempest blows;
It lifted waters of the sea;
Great rolling waves arose.

26 To heaven mounted ships
       and men,
    Then sank to depths again;
    Their souls were melted and
       were faint
    With fear and trouble then.
27 They staggered, reeled,
       like drunken men;
    No skill could they express.
28 In trouble to the LORD they cried;
    He saved them from distress.

29 The storm He changed into a calm
    By His command and will,
    And so the waves which
       raged before
    Now quiet were and still.
30 Then they were glad,
       because at rest
    And quiet was the sea.
    He led them to the haven thus
    Where they desired to be.

31 Let them give thanks unto
       the LORD
    For all His kindness shown.
    And for His works so wonderful
    Which He to men makes known.
32 Among the people where
       they meet
    Let them exalt His name.
    And where the elders have
       their seat
    Let them His praise proclaim.

Verses 33–43

33 He changes streams to wilderness
    And springs to thirsty ground,
34 A fruitful land to salty waste,
    When peoples' sins abound.
35 He turns the desert to a lake,
    Dry land to water springs,
36 And that they may prepare
       a home
37 The hungry there He brings.

They plant their vineyards, sow
    their fields;
Rich harvest there they grow;
38 His blessing makes them multiply,
    Their herds no decrease know.
39 Again they much diminished are
    And brought to low estate
    Through sorrow and adversity
    And through oppression great.

40 For He contempt on
       princes pours;
    He lets them go astray
    And wander in the wilderness
    Where there is not a way.
41 But He from trouble lifts the poor
    By setting them on high,
    And like a flock in families
    He makes them multiply.

42 When this the upright
       ones observe,
    They greatly shall rejoice,
    And all unrighteousness, ashamed,
    Shall cease to raise its voice.
43 Is any wise? He'll heed
       these things
    Which verses here record,
    And he'll consider well the love
    And kindness of the LORD.

TUNE: FOUNTAIN CMD (107D)
("There Is a Fountain")

Based on the *Book of Psalms,* 1871

93

Psalm 108

Verses 1–6

1 My heart is fixed, O God;
  I'll sing; my psalms I'll raise.
2 My soul shall sing; awake, O harp!
  At dawn I'll wake to praise.
3 I will give thanks to Thee
  Among the peoples, LORD.
  Among the nations of the world
  To Thee I'll psalms accord.

4 Above the heavens high
  Thy love and mercy rise;
  Thy faithfulness extendeth far;
  It reaches to the skies.
5 Be Thou exalted far
  Above the heav'ns, O God;
  And let Thy glory be advanced
  O'er all the earth abroad.

6 That Thy beloved ones
  Deliverance may see,
  O save us by Thy strong
    right hand;
  In mercy answer me.

Verses 7–13

7 God spoke in holiness;
  "I will exultant stand;
  From Shechem unto
    Succoth's vale
  I'll portion out the land.
8 For Gi-le-ad is Mine;
  Mine are Manasseh's fields;
  Yes, Ephraim defends My head;
  My scepter Judah wields.

9 "In Moab I will wash,
  My shoe on Edom throw;
  And o'er the land of Palestine
  In triumph I will go."
10 O who will bring me to
  The city fortified?
  Or who is he that to the land
  Of Edom will me guide?

11 Hast Thou not cast us off,
  O God, in Whom we boast?

Wilt Thou no more, O God,
    go forth
In battle with our host?
12 Against the foe give help;
  In vain the help man knows.
13 In God we shall do valiantly,
  For He'll tread down our foes.

TUNE: FESTAL SONG SM
(new *Trinity Hymnal*, p. 242)
("Rise Up O Men of God")

Elements from *The Psalter*, 1912

Psalm 109

Verses 1–12

1 God, my Praise, O be not silent!
2 Wicked and deceitful mouths
  Now are opened wide against me;
  Lying tongues against me speak.
3 They with hateful words
    beset me;
  They attack me without cause.
4 Spurning my love, they
    accuse me,
  Even while I pray for them.

5 So for good they pay me evil,
  Give me hatred for my love.
6 Set a wicked man against him,
  An accuser let him face.
7 When he's tried, let him be guilty;
  Let his prayer be counted sin.
8 May his days be few in number;
  May another seize his goods.

9 Without father be his children;
  May his wife a widow be.
10 May his children beg and wander,
  Driven from their ruined homes.
11 May the lender make him
    bankrupt;
  Strangers steal his hard-earned
    cash.
12 Let not one show kindness
    to him;
  Let none help his orphan sons!

13 His posterity be cut off!
   May none live to claim his name!
14 May the evil of his fathers
   Be recalled before the Lord.
   May no wrong deed of his mother
   From the record be erased.
15 May they all before
      the Lord stand,
   Pruned from earth their memory.

16 For he thought not to
      show mercy,
   But he persecuted still;
   And he chased the brokenhearted,
   Poor, and needy to their death.
17 He loved cursing; curses on him!
   He loathed blessing;
      give him none!
18 Like a coat he put on cursing;
   Water may it be to him.

   Let his cursing soak into him,
   Be like oil within his bones,
19 Like the garb he wraps
      around him,
   Like the belt he daily wears.
20 May this be to my accusers
   From the Lord their just reward;
   This to those who speak but evil,
   Who speak out against my life.

Verses 21–31

21 But may You, my God, Jehovah,
   Do for me for Your name's sake.
   Great in goodness is Your mercy!
   Rescue me in steadfast love.
22 I am very poor and needy;
   Stricken in me is my heart.
23 I am gone like ev'ning shadow,
   Like a locust shaken off.

24 Both my knees are weak
      from fasting;
   Gaunt my body has become.
25 Scorned am I by my accusers;
   Seeing me, they shake
      their heads.
26 Help me, O my God, Jehovah;

   Save me in Your mercy great.
27 Let them know that this is
      Your hand;
   You, O Lord, have done it all.

28 Let them curse me if You
      bless me.
   Let my foes be put to shame;
   But may gladness fill
      Your servant,
29 While dishonor covers them.
   Clothed with shame be
      my accusers,
   Wrapped up in their own
      disgrace.
30 With my mouth then will I offer
   Great thanksgiving to the Lord.

   In the midst of thronging people,
31 I will praise Him, for He stands
   At the right hand of the needy,
   Saving him from men of death.

TUNE: STUTTGART 87.87. (98B)
("God My King Thy Might Confessing")

Psalm 110

1 Jehovah to my Lord has said,
   "Sit Thou at My right hand
   Until I make Thy foes a stool
   Whereon Thy feet may stand."
2 Jehovah shall from Zion send
   The scepter of Thy power.
   In battle with Thine enemies
   Be Thou the conqueror.

3 A willing people in Thy day
   Of power shall come to Thee.
   Thy youth arrayed in holiness
   Like morning dew shall be.
4 Jehovah swore, and from His oath
   He never will depart:
   "Of th'order of Melchizedek
   A priest Thou ever art."

5 The Lord at Thy right hand
      shall smite
   Earth's rulers in His wrath.
6 Among the nations He shall judge;
   The slain shall fill His path.
   In many lands He'll overthrow
   Their kings with ruin dread;
7 And, marching, He'll drink from
      the brook
   And so lift up His head.

TUNE: ALL SAINTS NEW CMD (110)
("The Son of God Goes Forth to War")

Based on *Scottish Psalter*, 1650

Psalm 111

Verses 1–4

1 O praise the LORD! With all
      my heart
   Thanks to the LORD I'll bring,
   Where upright ones
      assembled are
   And congregations sing.
2 The works accomplished
      by the LORD
   Are very great in might.
   They are sought out by everyone
   Who finds in them delight.

3 His work displays the majesty
   And glory of His name,
   And His enduring righteousness
   Is evermore the same.
4 His works most wondrous
      He has made
   Remembered still to be.
   Jehovah is compassionate
   And merciful is He.

Verses 5–10

5 Those fearing Him He fills
      with food
   Provided by His hand.
   He keeps in mind His covenant,
   That it may ever stand.
6 He has the power of His works
   To His own people shown
   By giving them the heritage
   Of nations for their own.

7 His handiworks are truth
      and right;
   His precepts all are sure;
8 Set up in truth and uprightness,
   They ever shall endure.
9 He sent redemption to His folk,
10 His cov'nant did proclaim
   To last forever. Reverend
   And holy is His name.

The man who fears the LORD
has learned
The first of wisdom's ways.
They who obey will understand.
Forever lasts His praise.

TUNE: ST. MAGNUS CM (89D)
("The Head that Once was
Crowned with Thorns")

Elements from *Scottish Psalter*, 1650

Psalm 112

1 Praise to the LORD! The man is
blessed indeed
Who makes the LORD's commands
his great delight.
2 His children will be mighty
in the earth;
Descendants of the upright
will be blessed.

3 Abundant riches are within
his house;
His righteousness endures
forevermore.
4 The darkness of the just
will turn to light,
For all his ways are gracious,
kind and fair.

5 That man is good who gives
and freely lends,
And who with justice governs
his affairs.
6 The righteous man will never
be removed,
And ever will his mem-o-ry
endure.

7 At evil tidings he is not afraid;
His heart is steadfast, trusting
in the LORD.
8 His heart is steady; he will
never fear;
He comes at last to look
upon his foes.

9 With open hand he offers
to the poor;
His good endures; his head
is lifted high.
10 The wicked sees and grinds
his teeth in rage,
For he despairs; his cherished
hope must die.

TUNE: MORECOMBE 10.10.10.10. (18I)
("Spirit of God Descend")

Psalm 113

1 Praise Jehovah; praise the LORD;
Ye His servants, praise accord;
2 Bless-ed be Jehovah's name;
Evermore His praise proclaim.

3 From the dawn to setting sun,
Praise the LORD, the Mighty One.
4 O'er all nations He is high;
Yea, His glory crowns the sky.

5 Who is like the LORD our God?
High in heav'n is His abode,
6 Who Himself doth humble low
Things in heav'n and earth
to know.

7 He the lowly makes to rise
From the dust in which he lies,
8 That exalted he may stand
With the princes of the land.

9 He the childless woman takes
And a joyful mother makes;
Keeping house she finds reward.
Praise Jehovah; praise the LORD.

TUNE: MONKLAND 77.77.
(Old *Trinity Hymnal*, p. 30)
("Let Us with A Gladsome Mind") or
HENDON 77.77. (113A)
("Take My Life and Let It Be")

Psalm 114

1 When Isr'el had from
    Egypt gone,
Jacob from men of speech
    unknown;
2 Then Judah was His holy place,
And His dominion Isr'el's race.

3 The sea, affrighted, saw and fled;
Back Jordan driven was
    with dread;
4 The lofty mountains skipped
    like rams,
And all the little hills like lambs.

5 What ailed thee, that thou fledd'st,
    O sea?
Thou, Jordan, that thou back
    didst flee?
6 Ye mountains, that ye skipped
    like rams?
And all ye little hills like lambs?

7 O tremble, earth! The Lord is near:
Before the God of Jacob, fear;
8 Who from the rock did
    water bring,
And made the flint a waterspring.

TUNE: QUEBEC LM (HESPERUS) (119B)
("Jesus Thou Joy of Loving Hearts")

The *Book of Psalms*, 1871;
v. 7 altered 1994

Psalm 115

1 Not to us, LORD, not to us,
But to Your name glory give,
For Your steadfast love and grace,
For Your cov'nant faithfulness.
2 Why should heathen nations say,
"Where now is their mighty God?"

3 But our God in heaven is;
He does all that pleases Him;
4 Their gods are of silver, gold,
Fashioned by the hands of men:
5 They have mouths but
    do not speak;
They have eyes but do not see;

6 They have ears but do not hear,
Noses have but do not smell;
7 They have hands but
    do not touch;
They have feet but do not walk;
In their throat they
    make no sound.
8 Such, all who them make or trust.

9 Is-ra-el, trust in the LORD
He's their help and He's
    their shield!
10 Aaron's house, trust in the LORD
He's their help and He's
    their shield!
11 Who the LORD fear, trust the LORD
He's their help and He's
    their shield!

12 As the LORD has thought of us,
Mindful still, He'll bless us now,
He will bless all Isr'el's house;
He will bless all Aaron's house;
13 He'll bless all who fear the LORD
Whether they be small or great.

14 May the LORD so add to you
That your numbers will abound.
And as generations pass
May your children still increase.
15 Bless-ed be you of the LORD,
He Who made the heav'n
    and earth.

16 Heav'ns are heavens of the Lord,
Earth He's giv'n to sons of men.
17 Dead ones will not praise
the Lord,
Nor those bound for silent graves.
18 But we'll bless the Lord
henceforth,
Evermore. O praise the Lord!

TUNE: DIX 77.77.77.
(new *Trinity Hymnal*, p. 116)
("For the Beauty of the Earth")

Psalm 116

1 I love the Lord, because He hears
my pleading.
2 He's heeded me; through life I'll
call on Him.
3 The cords of death and Sheol's
terrors bound me;
In deep distress I grief and
trouble found.
4 Then on the Lord's name in
prayer I called:
"You I implore, O Lord, deliver
my soul!"

5 The Lord our God is merciful
and righteous;
6 Gracious, the Lord the simple
ones preserves.
When I was low, to me He
gave salvation.
7 Turn back again, my soul,
unto your rest,
8 Because the Lord has dealt
well with you,
Because my helpless soul You
rescued from death.

You saved my eyes from tears,
my feet from stumbling.
9 Before the Lord I'll walk in
lands of life.
10 I have believed and said,
"I am afflicted."
11 I in despair confessed,
"All men are false!"

12 What shall I render now to
the Lord
For all His benefits upon me
bestowed?
13 Salvation's cup I'll lift up in the
Lord's name,
14 Vows to the Lord before His
people pay.
15 Observed by Him and precious
in the Lord's sight
Appears the death of all His
saints each one.
16 O Lord, I am Your servant,
Your slave.
I am Your handmaid's son, for
You set me free.

17 To you I'll bring my off'ring of
thanksgiving;
With sacrifice I'll call upon
the Lord.
18 I'll pay the vows I made
unto Jehovah
Before His people all, O may
it be!
19 Within His courts, the house
of the Lord,
In midst of you, Jerusalem!
Praise the Lord!

TUNE: PILGRIMS 11.10.11.10.9.11. (116C)
("Hark, Hark, My Soul")

Psalm 117

First Version

1 From all that dwell below
   the skies,
  O let Jehovah's praise arise!
  Alleluia! Alleluia!
  And let His glorious name
   be sung
  In every land, by every tongue!
  Alleluia! Alleluia!

2 Great are the mercies of the Lord,
  And truth eternal is His word;
  Alleluia! Alleluia!
  Ye nations, sound from shore
   to shore
  Jehovah's praise for evermore!
  Alleluia! Alleluia!

TUNE: LAAST UNS ERFREUEN LM w/
ALLELUIA (new *Trinity Hymnal*, p. 115)
("All Creatures of Our God and King")

Isaac Watts, *The Psalms of David
Imitated*, 1719, as altered
in *Irish Psalter*, 1880

Psalm 117

Second Version

1 O all ye nations of the earth
  Give praises to the Lord;
  And all ye people magnify
  His name with one accord.

2 Because His lovingkindnesses
  Are mighty to-ward us;
  Jehovah's truth endures for aye.
  The Lord O do ye bless.

TUNE: ST. MARTIN'S CM (117A)

Based on the *Book of Psalms*, 1871

Psalm 118

Verses 1–16

1 O praise the LORD, for He is good;
   His steadfast love endures.
2 O let all Is-ra-el now say,
   "His steadfast love endures."
3 O let the house of Aaron say,
   "His steadfast love endures."
4 Let those that fear the LORD
      now say,
   "His steadfast love endures."

5 In my distress I sought the LORD;
   Jehovah answered me;
   He sent me in a spacious place,
   A place of liberty.
6 The mighty LORD is on my side;
   I will not be afraid;
   For anything that man can do
   I will not be dismayed.

7 The LORD is on my side with those
   Who render help to me.
   And so on all those hating me
   I my desire shall see.
8 O better far to trust the LORD
   Than rest in aid of men.
9 Yes, better far to trust the LORD
   Than rest in noblemen.

10 All nations have surrounded me;
   Their forces they deploy;
   But surely in Jehovah's name
   I will them all destroy.
11 Yes, they have all surrounded me,
   Surrounded to annoy;
   But surely in Jehovah's name
   I will them all destroy.

12 Though they surrounded me
      like bees,
   Like thorn fires soon they die,
   For surely in Jehovah's name
   Destroy them all will I.
13 Hard pressed, I was about to fall;
   The LORD gave help to me.
14 Jehovah is my strength and song
   And my salvation free.

15 Salvation's song and shouts of joy
   Are where the righteous dwells.
   The right hand of the mighty LORD
   In valiant deeds excels.
16 The right hand of the mighty LORD
   On high exalted is.
   The right hand of the mighty LORD
   In valiant deeds excels.

Verses 17–29

17 I shall not die, but live and tell
   Jehovah's power to save;
18 The LORD has sorely chastened me,
   But spared me from the grave.
19 O set ye open unto me
   The gates of righteousness;
   Then will I enter into them
   And I the LORD will bless.

20 This is Jehovah's gate; by it
   The just shall enter in.
21 I'll praise Thee Who hast heard my
      prayer,
   And hast my safety been.
22 That stone is made head
      cornerstone
   Which builders did despise.
23 This is the doing of the LORD,
   And wondrous in our eyes.

24 This is the day the LORD has made;
   Let us be glad and sing.
25 Hosanna, LORD! O give success!
   O LORD, salvation bring!
26 O bless-ed be the one who comes,
   Comes in Jehovah's name;
   The blessing from Jehovah's house
   Upon you we proclaim.

27 The LORD is God, and He to us
   Has made the light arise;
   O bind ye to the altar's horns
   With cords the sacrifice.
28 Thou art my God; I'll give
      Thee thanks.
   My God, I'll worship Thee.
29 O thank the LORD, for He is good;
   His grace will endless be.

TUNE: ST. ASAPH CMD (122A)

Based on *Scottish Psalter*, 1650

101

Psalm 119 – Part I

Aleph—Verses 1–8

1 How blest the blameless
in their way
Who from God's law do
not depart,
2 Who, holding fast the word
of truth,
Seek Him with undivided heart.
3 Yea, they are kept from paths
of sin
Who walk in His appointed way;
4 Thy precepts Thou hast given us
That we should faithfully obey.

5 My wav'ring heart is now resolved
Thy holy statutes to fulfill;
6 No more shall I be brought
to shame
When I regard Thy holy will.
7 To Thee my praise sincere
shall rise
When I Thy righteous judgments
learn;
8 Forsake me not, but be my guide,
And from Thy statutes I'll not turn.

Beth—Verses 9–16

9 How shall a young man
cleanse his way?
Let him with care Thy
word observe.
10 With all my heart I have
Thee sought;
From Thy commands let me
not swerve.
11 Thy word I've treasured
in my heart,
That I give no offense to Thee.
12 Thou, O Jehovah, bless-ed art;
Thy statutes teach Thou unto me.

13 I with my lips have oft declared
The judgments which Thy
mouth has shown,
14 More joy Thy testimonies gave
Than all the riches I have known.

15 I'll on Thy precepts meditate,
16 And have respect to all Thy ways.
I in Thy statutes will delight,
Thy word remember all my days.

TUNE: DUANE STREET LMD
(new *Trinity Hymnal*, p.148)
("How Shall the Young Direct")

Based on *The Psalter, 1912*

Psalm 119 – Part II

Gimmel—Verses 17–24

17 Do Thou in bounty deal with me,
Because I keep Thy way,
That by Thy favor I may live;
I will Thy word obey.
18 Unveil my eyes, that in Thy law
The wonders I may see.
19 I stranger am on earth; hide not
All Thy commands from me.

20 My soul is crushed because I for
Thine ordinances yearn.
21 Thou hast rebuked the proud,
accursed,
From Thy commands who turn.
22 Do Thou remove contempt
from me;
Take my reproach away;
For I Thy testimonies still
Observe and will obey.

23 The princes high against
me speak
Their counsel to fulfill,
But I, Thy servant, meditate
Upon Thy statutes still.
24 Thy testimonies also are
My comfort and delight;
They are as men who counsel me
And lead my steps aright.

Daleth—Verses 25–32

25 My soul has cleaved
    to dust; revive
According to Thy word.
26 Teach me Thy statutes;
    when my ways
I've told, Thou hast me heard.
27 Make me to know Thy
    precept's way,
Thy wonders to review.
28 My soul melts down with grief;
    my strength,
As Thou has said, renew.

29 The way of falsehood take
    from me;
Grant me Thy law in grace.
30 The faithful way I choose; I'll give
Thine ordinances place.
31 I to Thy testimonies cleave;
O LORD, no shame impart.
32 I'll run the way of Thy commands;
Thou wilt enlarge my heart.

He—Verses 33–40

33 Teach me, O LORD, Thy
    statutes' way;
I'll keep it to the end.
34 O make me wise; to keep Thy law
My whole heart shall attend.
35 Make me to follow Thy
    commands,
For they my joy maintain.
36 Thy testimonies claim my heart;
Keep me from love of gain.

37 Revive me in Thy way and turn
My eyes from vanity.
38 I am devoted to Thy fear;
Confirm Thy word to me.
39 Turn Thou away my feared
    reproach,
For good Thy judgments be.
40 Behold, I for Thy precepts longed;
In justice quicken me.

TUNE: STOCKTON CMD (20A)
("Only Trust Him")

Psalm 119 – Part III

Waw—Verses 41–48

41 O let Thy lovingkindnesses
Come unto me, O LORD.
May Thy salvation also come
According to Thy word.

42 Then I shall answer him
    who taunts,
For in Thy word I trust.
43 Take not from me the word
    of truth;
I wait Thy judgments just.

44 I'll keep forever, evermore,
The law which Thou dost speak.
45 And I will walk at liberty,
For I Thy precepts seek.

46 I'll of Thy testimonies speak
To kings and not be shamed.
47 In thy commandments which
    I love
I'll find the joy I've claimed.

48 To Thy commandments which
    I love
My hands I'll dedicate,
And in Thy statutes evermore
I'll deeply meditate.

Zayin—Verses 49–56

49 The promise keep in mind
    which Thou
Didst to Thy servant make,
The word which as a ground
    of hope
Thou causedst me to take.

50 By this in time of my distress
Great comfort I have known;
For in my straits I am revived
By this Thy word alone.

(Continues)

51 The men whose hearts with pride
        are filled
    Did greatly me deride;
    Yet from Thy good and holy law
    I have not turned aside.

52 Thy righteous judgments which
        Thou didst
    Make known of old, O LORD,
    I have remembered, and to me
    They comfort did afford.

53 Great wrath took hold of
        me because
    Ill men Thy law forsake.
54 I in my house of pilgrimage
    Thy laws my songs do make.

55 Thy name by night, LORD,
        I recalled,
    And I have kept Thy law.
56 And this I had because that I
    Thy precepts kept with awe.

Heth — Verses 57–64

57 The LORD my portion is; I've said
    I'll keep Thy words to me.
58 I've sought Thy face with all
        my heart;
    As promised, gracious be.

59 I viewed my ways, turned my
        feet toward
    Thy testimonies' way.
60 I hastened Thy commands
        to keep;
    My feet made no delay.

61 The wicked wrapped me 'round
        with cords;
    Thy law I did not slight.
62 I'll rise at midnight, thanking Thee
    For all Thy judgments right.

63 I'm with those who Thy
        precepts keep
    And all those fearing Thee.
64 Thy mercy fills the earth, O LORD;
    Thy statutes teach Thou me.

Teth — Verses 65–72

65 According to Thy word, O LORD,
    Thou hast Thy servant blessed.
66 Teach me good judgment,
        knowledge give;
    On Thy commands I rest.

67 Ere I afflicted was I strayed;
    Thy word I now obey.
68 For good Thou art and
        doest good;
    Teach me Thy statutes' way.

69 The proud besmear with lies,
        but I
    Thy precepts keep aright.
70 Their heart is buried deep in fat;
    Thy law is my delight.

71 It has been very good for me.
    That I was humbled low.
    It through affliction was that I
    Thy statutes came to know.

72 The law proceeding from
        Thy mouth
    I much more precious hold
    Than countless thousands of
        fine coins
    Of silver and of gold.

Yodh — Verses 73–80

73 Thy hands created me;
        make wise,
    All Thy commands to learn.
74 May those who fear Thee see
        with joy
    How to Thy word I turn.

75 I know, O LORD, that righteous are
    Thy judgments one and all,
    And that in faithfulness Thou hast
    Let trouble on me fall.

76 O let Thy steadfast love cheer me,
    As promised to Thy slave.
77 May Thy compassion bring
        me life;
    Thy law great pleasure gave.

78 O may the arrogant be shamed
Who falsely me accuse
To overturn me; yet I shall
Upon Thy precepts muse.

79 To me all turn, who, fearing Thee,
Thy testimonies claim.
80 Let my heart in Thy statutes be
United, without shame.

TUNE: ST. PETER CM (37F)
("In Christ There Is No East or West")

vv. 49–56, 73–80,
The Book of Psalms with Music, 1950

Psalm 119 – Part IV

Kaph — Verses 81–88

81 My soul for Thy salvation faints;
Yet I Thy word believe.
82 Mine eyes are failing for
Thy word;
When wilt Thou comfort give?
83 For like a wineskin I'm become
That in the smoke is set;
But yet the statutes Thou
hast giv'n
I never will forget.

84 How many are Thy servant's
days;
When wilt Thou execute
Just judgment on these
wicked men
That do me persecute?
85 The proud have digged a pit
for me;
They disregard Thy laws;
86 Thy words all faithful are;
help me,
Pursued without a cause.

87 They so consumed me that
on earth
My life they scarce did leave;
Thy precepts yet forsook I not
But close to them did cleave.
88 According to Thy love and grace
Me quicken and preserve;
The testimony of Thy mouth
So shall I still observe.

Lamed — Verses 89–96

89 For evermore in heav'n, O LORD,
Thy word is settled fast;
90 Thy truth extends to every age;
Thou mad'st the earth to last.
91 Thy laws continue to this day;
To Thee all things give heed.
92 If in Thy law I found no joy,
I'd perish in deep need.

93 Thy precepts I will ne'er forget;
They quick'ning to me brought.
94 For I am Thine; O save Thou me;
Thy precepts I have sought.
95 The wicked seek my death, but I
Thy testimonies laud.
96 Of all perfection bounds I've seen,
For Thy command is broad.

Mem — Verses 97–104

97 O how I love Thy law; it is
My study all the day.
98 It makes me wiser than my foes;
Its precepts with me stay.
99 More than my teachers or the old
Thy servant understands;
Thy testimonies I consult
100 And follow Thy commands.

101 I stayed my feet from evil ways
That I Thy word observe;
102 I have been taught by Thee
and from
Thy judgments will not swerve.
103 How sweet in taste Thy promises,
Than honey far more sweet!
104 Thy precepts understanding give;
I therefore hate deceit.
(Turn page for next section)

105 Thy word is to my feet a lamp,
And to my path a light.
106 I sworn have, and I will confirm
To keep Thy judgments right.
107 I'm humbled much; LORD,
quicken me
According to Thy word.
108 Accept the off'rings of my mouth;
Teach me Thy judgments, LORD.

109 My soul is ever in my hand;
Thy law I never spurn.
110 The wicked laid a snare, yet from
Thy precepts I'll not turn.
111 I'm to Thy testimonies heir;
They joy to my heart lend.
112 My heart Thy statutes longs
to keep
Forever to the end.

TUNE: BETHLEHEM CMD (149)

vv. 81-88,
The Book of Psalms with Music, 1950

Samech—Verses 113–120

113 The men of double mind I hate;
Thy law my love has stirred!
114 Thou art my shield and
hiding place;
My hope is in Thy word.

115 Depart, illdoers, that I may
My God's commandments heed.
116 Sustain as Thou hast promised me
That I may live indeed.

117 Quench not my hope, but hold
me safe;
Thy statutes I'll respect.
118 All those who from Thy
statutes err,
In scorn Thou dost reject.

How useless their deceitfulness!
In falsehood is no gain.
119 Thou dost the wicked purge
from earth
Like dross, that none remain.

120 So I Thy testimonies love
My flesh is quivering
For fear of Thee; and deepest awe
Thy judgments surely bring.

Ayin—Verses 121–128

121 To others I have judgment done,
Performing what is right;
O do not then deliver me
To my oppressor's might.

122 Be surety for Thy servant's good;
From proud oppressors free;
123 Thy saving help and
righteous word
My failing eyes would see.

124 In mercy with Thy servant deal;
Thy statutes to me show;
125 I am Thy servant; wisdom give
That I Thy laws may know.

126 'Tis time Thou work, O LORD,
for they
Make void Thy law divine.
127 Thy precepts therefore more
I love
Than gold, yea, gold most fine.

128 Concerning all things Thy
commands
I therefore judge are right;
And ev'ry false and wicked way
Is hateful in my sight.

TUNE: MEDITATION CM (13)

vv. 121-128,
The Book of Psalms with Music, 1950;

Psalm 119 – Part VI

Pe—Verses 129–136

129 Your testimonies I observe,
For they are wondrous in
my eyes.
130 The op'ning of Your word gives
light,
And makes the simplehearted
wise.
131 I open wide my mouth and pant
For all commandments
You proclaim.
132 O turn to me! Deal graciously
As to all those who love
Your name.

133 My steps establish in Your word
And let no sin o'er me have sway.
134 Redeem me from the power
of man,
And I Your precepts will obey.
135 Your face make on Your servant
shine;
Teach me Your statutes;
for I weep;
136 The tears in streams flow from
my eyes,
Because your law they do
not keep.

Tsadhe—Verses 137–144

137 You ever righteous are, O LORD;
And all Your judgments upright
stand.
138 Your righteous testimonies all
You do in faithfulness command.
139 By zeal I am consumed, because
Your words my adversaries spurn.
140 Your promise is so very pure.
Toward it Your servant loves
to turn.

141 Though I am small and
much despised,
Your precepts I do not forget
142 Eternal is Your righteousness;
Your law in truth is firmly set,
143 Distress and anguish have
me found,
Yet joy by Your commands
You give.
144 Your testimonies righteous are;
O make me wise that I may live.

Qoph—Verses 145–152

145 My heart cries out! LORD,
answer me!
And I your statutes will obey.
146 O save me, for I've called to You;
Your testimonies I'll display.
147 I rose before the dawn and cried;
For by Your word my hope
is stirred.
148 I wake throughout the hours
of night
To meditate upon Your word.

149 In mercy listen to my voice;
In judgment, LORD, my life renew.
150 Those plotting ill draw ever near,
Far from Your law their
way pursue.
151 But You, O LORD, are ever near,
And true are all of Your
commands.
152 Your testimonies make me sure
That what You say forever stands.

(Turn page for next section)

153 Regard my grief and rescue me,
   For I Your law do not forget.
154 Defend my cause and me redeem;
   Your promise keep; revive me yet.
155 Salvation's far from wicked men;
   Your statutes they'll not try to see.
156 How many are Your mercies, LORD!
   In judgments just give life to me.

157 My persecutors many are,
   Your testimonies I'll not spurn.
158 I saw the faithless and
      was grieved,
   For to Your word they
      won't return.
159 Behold how I Your precepts love!
   In mercy, LORD, give life to me.
160 The sum of all Your words
      is truth;
   Your judgments stand eternally.

Shin—Verses 161–168

161 The princes causelessly pursue;
   But words from You my
      heart reveres.
162 I at Your promise joy as one
   For whom abundant spoil appears.
163 I falsehood hate and lies abhor;
   But in Your law is my delight.
164 I praise You seven times a day
   Because your judgments all are
      right.

165 Great peace have those who
      love Your law;
   For them there is no stumbling
      block.
166 I hope for Your salvation, LORD,
   And I in Your commandments
      walk.
167 My soul Your testimonies keeps
   And deeply loves; my heart obeys
168 Your precepts, testimonies all,
   Because before You are my ways.

169 Before You let my cry come near,
   O LORD; true to Your word,
      teach me.
170 Before You let my pleading come;
   True to Your promise rescue me.
171 My lips are breaking forth
      in praise;
   Teach me Your statutes
      to confess.
172 My tongue gives answer
      to Your word,
   For Your commands are
      righteousness.

173 Be ready with Your hand to help,
   Because Your precepts are
      my choice.
174 I long for Your salvation, LORD,
   And ever in Your law rejoice.
175 My soul shall live with praise
      to You;
   My need for help Your
      judgments met.
176 A straying sheep, Your
      servant seek,
   For Your commands I ne'er forget.

TUNE: GUIDANCE LMD
("He Leadeth Me")
(new *Trinity Hymnal*, p. 600)

vv. 129–136, 145–160, 169–176,
The Book of Psalms with Music, 1950;
vv. 137–152 and 161–168, *The Book of
Psalms for Singing*, 1973.
Altered 1994

Psalm 120

1 I cried in trouble to the LORD,
    And He has answered me.
2 From lying lips and crafty tongue,
    O LORD, my soul set free.

3 What shall be given you,
        false tongue?
    What added to your doom?
4 Sharp arrows of a mighty man,
    And redhot coals of broom.

5 Alas for me, that I sojourn
    So long in Meshech's land,
    That I have made my
        dwelling where
    The tents of Kedar stand!

6 Too long my soul has made
        its home
    With those who peace abhor.
7 I am for peace, but when I speak
    They ready are for war.

TUNE: WINDSOR CM
(new *Trinity Hymnal*, p. 27)
("Great God How Infinite")

Psalm 121

1 I to the hills will lift my eyes.
    From whence shall come my aid?
2 My safety cometh from the LORD
    Who heav'n and earth has made.

3 Thy foot He'll not let slide,
        nor will
    He slumber that thee keeps.
4 Lo, He that keepeth Is-ra-el,
    He slumbers not nor sleeps.

5 The LORD thee keeps; the LORD
        thy shade
    On thy right hand doth stay;
6 The moon by night thee shall
        not smite,
    Nor yet the sun by day.

7 The LORD shall keep thee
        from all ill;
    He shall preserve thy soul.
8 The LORD as thou shalt go
        and come
    Forever keeps thee whole.

TUNE: DUNDEE CM (28A)

Based on *Scottish Psalter*, 1650

109

Psalm 122

1 I was glad to hear them saying,
  "To the LORD's house let us go."
2 For our feet will soon be standing
  In your gates, Jerusalem,
3 Salem, well constructed city;
4 There assemble all the tribes,
  Tribes that are Jehovah's own.

  This the ordinance for Isr'el,
  Here to thank Jehovah's name.
5 There are set the thrones
     of judgment;
  There is David's house enthroned.
6 Pray then for the peace of Salem;
  May they prosper who love you.
7 Be there peace within your walls.

8 In your palaces be safety.
  For the sake of brothers all,
  For the sake of my companions,
9 I am saying, "Peace to you!"
  For Jehovah's house within you,
  Temple of the LORD our God,
  I will ever seek your good.

TUNE: CWM RHONDDA 87.87.877.
       (122B)
("Guide Me O Thou Great Jehovah")

Psalm 123

1 To Thee I lift my eyes, O Thou
  Who art in heav'n enthroned.
2 As servants watch their
     master's hand,
  Or as a maid's eyes wait
  Her mistress' hand to see,

  So our eyes, waiting, now attend
  Upon the LORD our God,
  Until He gracious be to us.
3 Be gracious to us, LORD.
  Be gracious unto us.

  For we are sated with contempt;
  Our soul is surfeited
4 With all the scoffing insolence
  Of those who live at ease,
  And with the proud's contempt.

TUNE: CHRISTMAS 86.866.
(new *Trinity Hymnal*, p. 223)
("While Shepherds Watched")

Psalm 124

1 Now Is-ra-el may say and that
   in truth,
"If that the LORD had not our
   right maintained,
2 If that the LORD had not with
   us remained,
When cruel men against us
   rose to strive,
3 We surely had been
   swallowed up alive.

Yea, when their wrath against
   us fiercely rose,
4 Then as fierce floods before them
   all things drown,
So had they brought our soul
   to death quite down;
5 The raging streams, with their
   proud swelling waves,
Had then our soul o'erwhelmed
   as in the grave."

6 Blessed be the LORD Who made us
   not their prey;
7 As from the snare a bird
   escapeth free,
Their net is rent and so escaped
   are we.
8 Our only help is in Jehovah's
   name,
Who made the earth and all
   the heav'nly frame.

TUNE: OLD 124TH 10.10.10.10.10.
(124B)

Based on William Whittingham and
   Scottish Psalter, 1564,
   and *The Psalter*, 1912

Psalm 125

1 Like Zion's mountain shall they be
Who in the LORD confide,
A mount which never can
   be moved
But ever shall abide.

2 As all around Jerusalem
The mountains firmly stand,
The LORD for evermore surrounds
The people of His hand.

3 Upon the land of righteous ones
No evil rule shall press,
Lest righteous men put forth
   their hands
To work unrighteousness.

4 O LORD, to those men who
   are good
Show Yourself good and kind,
And likewise show Your
   goodness to
All them of upright mind.

5 Yet shall the LORD drive out
   all those
In crooked ways who dwell,
Along with all who practice sin;
But peace on Is-ra-el!

TUNE: WINCHESTER OLD CM (78B) or
ABBEYVILLE (125)

Elements from *The Psalter*, 1912

Psalm 126

1 When Zion's exile band
The LORD brought back, we were
As those who dream.
2 For then our mouth was filled
With laughter and delight;
Our tongue then overflowed
With shouts of joy.

Among the nations all
They said, "The LORD has done
Great things for them!"
3 The LORD has done for us
Great things, and we are glad.
4 Restore our fortunes, LORD,
Like desert streams.

5 For those who sow in tears
Shall reap at harvest time
With shouts of joy.
6 The one who weeping goes,
Bearing his precious seed,
Shall singing come again,
Bearing his sheaves.

TUNE: OLIVETTE 664.66.64.
(new *Trinity Hymnal*, p. 528)
("My Faith Looks Up to Thee")

Psalm 127

1 Except the LORD shall build
the house
The builders lose their pain;
Except the LORD the city keep
The watchmen watch in vain.

2 'Tis vain for you to rise betimes,
Or late from rest to keep,
To eat the bread of toil; for so
He gives His loved ones sleep.

3 Lo, children are the LORD's
good gift;
Rich payment are men's sons.
4 The sons of youth as arrows are
In hands of mighty ones.

5 Who has his quiver filled
with these,
O happy shall he be;
When foes they greet within
the gate
They shall from shame be free.

TUNE: GLASGOW CM (100B)

Based on *Scottish Psalter*, 1650

Psalm 128

1 Blessed the man that fears
Jehovah
And that walketh in His ways;
2 Thou shalt eat of thy hands' labor
And be prospered all thy days.
3 Like a vine with fruit abounding
In thy house thy wife is found,
And like olive plants thy children,
Compassing thy table round.

4 Lo, on him that fears Jehovah
Shall this blessedness attend;
5 For Jehovah out of Zion
Shall to thee His blessing send.
Thou shalt see Jerus'lem prosper
All thy days till life shall cease;
6 Thou shalt see thy children's
children,
Unto Is-ra-el be peace.

TUNE: NETTLETON 87.87.D (119Q)
("Come, Thou Fount of Every Blessing")

Based on the *Book of Psalms*, 1871 and
The Psalter, 1912

112

Psalm 129

1 "Time and again they greatly did
    oppress me
  From my youth up," let Is-ra-el
    declare;
2 "Time and again they greatly did
    oppress me
  From my youth up, yet they did
    not prevail."

3 Upon my back, like plowmen
    plowing furrows,
  So did they make their gouges
    deep and long.
4 Yet is Jehovah righteous in His
    dealings;
  The ropes of lawless men He
    cuts apart.

5 Let them be shamed and fall back
    in confusion,
  All those who bear for Zion
    bitter hate.
6 Let them become like grass upon
    the housetops
  Which withers up before it can
    be pulled.

7 From such the reaper cannot get
    one hand full,
  Nor can the one who binds fill up
    his arms.
8 None passing say, "Jehovah's
    blessing on you!
  We give you blessing in
    Jehovah's name!"

TUNE: OLD 110TH 11.10.11.10. (129)

Psalm 130

1 Lord, from the depths to Thee
    I cried.
2 My Lord, give ear to me.
  O hear my voice and hearken to
  My supplicating plea.

3 Lord, who shall stand if Thou,
    my Lord,
  Shouldst mark iniquity?
4 But yet with Thee forgiveness is,
  That men may rev'rence Thee.

5 I wait, my soul awaits the Lord;
  My hope is in His word.
6 More than the watchmen wait
    for morn
  My soul waits for my Lord.

7 O Is-ra-el, hope in the Lord;
  The Lord saves graciously.
8 And He shall Is-ra-el redeem
  From all iniquity.

TUNE: MARTYRDOM CM (90A)
("Alas and Did My Savior Bleed")

Based on *Scottish Psalter,* 1650

Psalm 131

1 My heart not haughty is, O Lord,
  Nor lofty is my eye;
  I do not deal in matters great
  Or things for me too high.

2 My soul I stilled and quieted.
  I'm like a weaned child;
  As one that to his mother yields
  With soul subdued and mild.

3 Upon Jehovah let the hope
  Of Is-ra-el rely,
  Ev'n from the time that present is
  To all eternity.

TUNE: DUNFERMLINE CM (8A)
("Almighty God, Your Seed is Cast")

Based on *Scottish Psalter,* 1650

Psalm 132

Verses 1–10

1 David, and all his anxious care,
　Do Thou, O Lord, remember now;
2 How he unto the Lord did swear,
　To Jacob's Mighty One did vow:

3 "Into my house I will not go,
　Nor will I on my bed repose;
4 Sleep to mine eyes I will
　　not know,
　Slumber shall not mine
　　eyelids close;

5 "Till I a place find for the Lord,
　A house for Jacob's Strong
　　One build."
6 Of it at Ephratah we heard,
　We found it in the forest-field.

7 We'll go into His courts, and bow
　Before the footstool of His grace.
8 Arise, Thine ark of strength,
　　and Thou,
　O Lord, into Thy resting place.

9 O clothe Thy priests with
　　righteousness,
　And let Thy saints glad
　　shoutings make;
10 Avert not Thine anointed's face,
　For Thine own servant
　　David's sake.

Verses 11–18

11 The Lord hath unto David sworn
　In truth, He will not turn from it,
　"I of the sons unto thee born
　Will make upon thy throne to sit.

12 "If they My cov'nant will obey,
　And testimonies I make known,
　Their children I will bless,
　　and they
　Shall sit for ever on thy throne."

13 The Lord hath chosen Zion hill;
　For there He hath desired
　　to dwell.
14 "This is My rest, and here I will
　Abide; for I do like it well.

15 "I'll her provision richly bless;
　With bread her poor I'll satisfy;
16 Her priests I'll clothe with
　　righteousness;
　Her saints with shouts of joy
　　shall cry.

17 "To bud I'll there make
　　David's horn,
　And for My king a lamp I'll trim;
18 His enemies I'll clothe with scorn,
　But flourish shall his crown
　　on him."

TUNE: FEDERAL STREET LM (119W)

Irish Psalter, 1880; altered 1994.

Psalm 133

1 Behold how good a thing it is,
　And how becoming well,
　When those that brethren
　　are delight
　In unity to dwell.

2 For it is like the precious oil
　Poured out on Aaron's head,
　That, going down upon his beard,
　Upon his garments spread.

3 Like Hermon's dew upon the hills
　Of Zion that descends,
　The Lord commands His
　　blessing there,
　Ev'n life that never ends.

TUNE: AZMON CM (133A)
("O, For a Thousand Tongues to Sing")

Based on *Scottish Psalter*, 1650

114

Psalm 134

1 Lo, with praises to Jehovah,
Blessing give with one accord,
All of you who faithful service
To Jehovah do afford,
Standing serving Him each night
In the dwelling of the LORD.

2 Toward His holy sanctuary
Let your hands be lifted high
To give blessing to Jehovah.
And from Zion in reply
May Jehovah blessing give
He Who made the earth and sky.

TUNE: ALL SAINTS OLD 87.87.77.
(old *Trinity Hymnal*, p.127)
("Let Us Love and Sing and Wonder")

Altered. 1993

Psalm 135

1 Hallelujah! Praise the LORD's name!
Praise Him, servants of the LORD,
2 You that in the LORD's house serve
Him,
In God's courtyard standing
guard.
3 Praise the LORD! How good the
LORD is!
Sing His name—how sweet
its tone!
4 For the LORD has chosen Jacob,
Is-ra-el to be his own.

5 Well I know how great the LORD
is;
Our Lord is above all gods.
6 For the LORD does what He
pleases
In all heav'n, earth, deeps, and
floods.
7 He it is Who lifts the vapors
From the ends of earth and sea,
Who with lightnings brings the
rain down,
From His store the wind sets free,

8 Who slew all of Egypt's firstborn,
9 On you, Egypt, wonders sent.
Signs to Pharaoh and his servants,
10 Who killed kings, their
kingdoms rent
11 Mighty Sihon, Og of Bashan,
Then the Kings of Canaan fell!
12 God their land gave to His
people,
Willed it all to Is-ra-el.

13 Your name, LORD, endures
forever;
Your fame, LORD, each age has
known;
14 For the LORD acquits His people,
Has compassion on His own.
15 Heathen idols, gold and silver,
Work of human artistry:
16 Having mouths, they speak of
nothing;
Having eyes, they do not see.

17 Having ears, they never hearken;
They do not breathe out or in.
18 Those who make them will be
like them,
All whose trust in them has been.
19 Bless the LORD, O house of Is-r'el!
House of Aaron, bless the LORD!
20 Bless the LORD, O house of Levi!
All who fear Him, bless the LORD!

Blessings to the LORD you worship!
21 Blessed from Zion be the LORD,
He whose dwelling is in Salem!
Hallelujah! Praise the LORD!
1 *Hallelujah! Praise the LORD's name!*
Praise Him, servants of the LORD,
2 *You that in the LORD's house serve*
Him,
In God's courtyard standing
guard.

TUNE: KIRKPATRICK 87.87.D (135B)

115

Psalm 136

Verses 1–16

1 O thank the LORD, for good is He;
His mercy lasts forever.
2 Thanks to the God of gods
give ye;
His mercy lasts forever.
3 O praises give the King of kings;
His mercy lasts forever;
4 For He alone does wondrous
things;
His mercy lasts forever;

5 Who in His wisdom framed
the skies;
His mercy lasts forever;
6 Who made the earth from
waters rise;
His mercy lasts forever;
7 Who placed the great lights
on display;
His mercy lasts forever;
8 The sun to rule the sky by day;
His mercy lasts forever;

9 The moon and stars to rule
the night;
His mercy lasts forever;
10 Who Egypt's firstborn all
did smite;
His mercy lasts forever;
11 Who freed all Isr'el from
their charm;
His mercy lasts forever;
12 With mighty hand and outstretched
arm;
His mercy lasts forever;

13 Who by His wind the Red Sea
clave;
His mercy lasts forever;
14 Led Isr'el through the parted wave;
His mercy lasts forever;
15 O'er Pharaoh He the Red Sea
spread;
His mercy lasts forever;
16 Through desert wastes His
people led;
His mercy lasts forever;

Verses 17–26, 3–4

17 To Him Who great kings
overthrew;
His mercy lasts forever;
18 Who famous kings in battle slew;
His mercy lasts forever;
19 King Sihon, of the Amorites;
His mercy lasts forever;
20 And Og, the king of Bashanites;
His mercy lasts forever;

21 Their land He gave to Is-ra-el;
His mercy lasts forever;
22 His servant gave a place to dwell;
His mercy lasts forever.
23 He thought on us when
we were low;
His mercy lasts forever;
24 And made us free from every foe;
His mercy lasts forever.

25 He food bestows on all that live;
His mercy lasts forever.
26 Thanks to the God of
heaven give;
His mercy lasts forever.
3 *O praises give the King of kings;*
His mercy lasts forever;
4 *For He alone does wondrous*
things;
His mercy lasts forever.

TUNE: CONSTANCE 87.87.D (136B)
("I've Found a Friend")

Based on John Craig and
Scottish Psalter, 1564

116

Psalm 137

1 By Babel's streams we sat
 and wept;
 Our thoughts to Zion turned.
2 There on its willow trees we hung
 Our harps which now we
 spurned.
3 For there a song demanded they
 Who did us captive bring,
 And our tormentors called
 for mirth:
 "A song of Zion sing!"

4 O how the LORD's song shall
 we sing
 Within a foreign land?
5 If you, Jerus'lem, I forget,
 Let wither my right hand.
6 Let my tongue cleave to
 my mouth's roof
 If you I should forget,
 And if above my chiefest joy
 I Salem do not set.

7 Remember Edom's sons, O LORD,
 How in Jerus'lem's day
 They cried, "Tear down!
 Tear down its walls!
 Its base in ruins lay!"
8 O Babel's daughter, near
 your doom,
 O happy count that one
 Who shall deal back to you again
 As you to us have done!

9 Yes, happy count that one
 who adds
 To your destruction's shock,
 Who takes and breaks your
 little ones
 Against the mighty rock.

TUNE: NAOMI CM (22A)
("Father, Whate'er of Earthly Bliss")

Based on *Scottish Psalter*, 1650

Psalm 138

1 With all my heart my
 thanks I'll bring,
 Before the gods Thy praises sing;
2 I'll worship in Thy holy place
 And praise Thy name for
 truth and grace;

 For Thou above Thy name adored
 Hast magnified Thy faithful word.
3 The day I called Thy
 help appeared;
 With inward strength my
 soul was cheered.

4 All kings of earth shall
 thanks accord
 When they have heard Thy
 words, O LORD;
5 Jehovah's ways they'll celebrate;
 The glory of the LORD is great.

6 Although Jehovah is most high,
 On lowly ones He bends His eye;
 But those that proud and
 haughty are
 He knoweth only from afar.

7 Through trouble though my
 pathway be,
 Thou wilt revive and comfort me.
 Thine outstretched hand Thou
 wilt oppose
 Against the wrath of all my foes.

 Thy hand, O LORD, shall set
 me free
8 And perfect what concerneth me;
 Thy mercy, LORD, forever stands;
 Leave not the work of Thine own
 hands.

TUNE: HURSLEY LM (138A)
("Sun of My Soul") or
WESLEY LM (138B)

Psalm 139

Verses 1–12

1 Lord, Thou hast searched me;
2   Thou hast known
My rising and my sitting down;
And from afar Thou knowest well
The very thoughts that in
   me dwell.

3 Thou knowest all the ways I plan,
My path and lying down
   dost scan;
4 For in my tongue no word can be,
But, lo, O Lord, 'tis known
   to Thee.

5 Behind, before me, Thou dost
   stand
And lay on me Thy mighty hand;
6 Such knowledge is for me
   too strange
And high beyond my
   utmost range.

7 Where shall I from Thy Spirit flee,
Or from Thy presence hidden be?
8 In heav'n Thou art, if there I fly,
In death's abode, if there I lie.

9 If I the wings of morning take
And utmost sea my
   dwelling make,
10 Ev'n there Thy hand shall
   guide my way
And Thy right hand shall
   be my stay.

11 If I say, "Darkness covers me,"
12 The darkness hideth not
   from Thee.
To Thee both night and day
   are bright;
The darkness shineth as the light.

13 My inward parts were formed
   by Thee;
Within the womb, Thou
   fashioned me;
14 And I Thy praises will proclaim,
For strange and wondrous
   is my frame.

Thy wondrous works I
   surely know;
15 When as in depths of earth below
My frame in secret first was made,
'Twas all before Thine eyes
   displayed.

16 Mine unformed substance
   Thou didst see;
The days that were ordained
   to me
Were written in Thy book,
   each one,
When as of them there yet
   was none.

17 Thy thoughts, O God, to me
   are dear;
18 How great their sum! They
   more appear
In number than the sand to me.
When I awake, I'm still with Thee.

19 The wicked Thou wilt slay,
   O God;
Depart from me, ye men of blood,
20 They speak of Thee in
   words profane,
The foes who take Thy name
   in vain.

21 Do not I hate Thy foes, O Lord?
And thine assailants hold
   abhorred?
22 I truly hate all foes of Thine;
I count them enemies of mine.

23 Search me, O God;
    my heart discern;
  And try me, every thought
    to learn,
24 And see if any sin holds sway.
  Lead in the everlasting way.

TUNE: MARYTON LM (139B)
("O Master Let Me Walk")

Based on the *Book of Psalms*, 1871;
vs. 13 altered 1994

Psalm 140

1 From men of greed and violence,
  O Lord, my soul release;
2 They evil in their hearts devise,
  And wars they would increase.
3 As keen as any serpent's fangs
  So sharp their tongues they make,
  And underneath their lips
    there hides
  The venom of a snake.

4 Guard me from men of violence,
  O Lord, from lawless force;
  Their purpose is to bring
    me down,
  To overthrow my course.
5 The proud hid traps and cords
    for me;
  They have a secret net
  Along the wayside spread for me,
  And snares for me they set.

6 But I have said unto the Lord,
  "In truth my God art Thou."
  Jehovah, hear my voice when I
  In supplication bow.
7 My Lord Jehovah is for me
  Salvation's strength and stay;
  He is the cover for my head
  When comes the battleday.

8 Grant not, O Lord, that
    wicked men
  See their desire draw nigh.
  And do not help them in
    their plots

  To lift themselves on high.
9 As for the head of all those men
  Who have surrounded me,
  By all the mischief of their lips
  Let them now covered be.

10 Let burning coals upon them fall;
  To flames let them be cast,
  And into deepest pits from which
  They cannot rise at last.
11 Let not the slanderer on earth
  Enjoy security;
  Let evil hunt the violent
  And smite relentlessly.

12 I know Jehovah will maintain
  The cause of those oppressed;
  He will defend the right of those
  By poverty distressed.
13 And then the righteous to
    Thy name
  Their thanks will surely give;
  And they that upright are in heart
  Shall in Thy presence live.

TUNE: HALIFAX CM (89E)

Psalm 141

1 O LORD, My God, to Thee I cry;
  Swift to my aid in mercy fly;
  And when to Thee my
      cries ascend,
  In pity to my voice attend.
2 As fragrant incense on the air,
  So mount to heav'n my
      early prayer;
  And let my hands uplifted be,
  As evening sacrifice to Thee.

3 Set, LORD, a watch my
      mouth before,
  And of my lips keep Thou
      the door;
4 Nor leave my sinful heart to stray
  Where evil footsteps lead the way.
  Let me not of the feast partake
  Which wicked men delight
      to make;
5 Let righteous men in mercy smite,
  In their reproofs I'll take delight.

  Let righteous lips my errors chide,
  Like healing oil the accents glide;
  If voice of faithful friend reprove,
  Such smiting comes to me in love.
  For them, when they are
      in distress,
  To God I will my prayer address;
6 Their judges cast on rocky ground,
  Then sweet to them my words
      shall sound.

7 Around the graves our bones
      are left,
  As branches by the woodman cleft.
8 To Thee, Lord GOD, I lift my eyes;
  On Thee my helpless soul relies.
9 Preserve me from the secret net,
  The toils which im-pious hands
      have set;
10 In their own snares let sinners fall,
  While I by grace escape them all.

TUNE: CANONBURY LM (18C)
("Lord Speak to Me that I May Speak")

Book of Psalms, 1871

Psalm 142

1 Unto the LORD my voice I raise,
  Unto the LORD my voice
      now prays;
2 Before His face my grief I show
  And tell my trouble and my woe.

3 When gloom and sorrow
      compass me,
  The path I take is known to Thee,
  So are the snares that foes do lay
  To snare Thy servant in his way.

4 All unprotected, lo, I stand,
  No friendly guar-dian at my hand,
  No place of flight or refuge near,
  And none to whom my soul
      is dear.

5 O LORD, my Saviour, now to Thee,
  Without a hope beside, I flee,
  To Thee, my shelter from
      the strife,
  My portion in the land of life.

6 Be Thou my help when
      troubles throng,
  For I am weak and foes
      are strong;
7 My captive soul from prison bring,
  And thanks to Thy name
      I will sing.

  The righteous then shall
      gather round
  To share the blessing
      I have found,
  Their hearts made glad
      because they see
  How richly Thou hast dealt
      with me.

TUNE: ROCKINGHAM OLD LM (145C)

Based on the *Book of Psalms,* 1871 and
  The Psalter, 1912; altered 1994

120

Psalm 143

1 LORD, hearken to my prayer;
My supplication hear.
Reply in truth and in
righteousness.
2 And with Your servant now
To judgment do not come,
For in Your sight no man is just.

3 The foe has hounded me;
My life to earth he crushed.
Entombed he kept me as those
long dead.
4 My spirit therefore faints,
Within me overwhelmed.
My heart in me is desolate.

5 I days of old recall;
I muse on all Your deeds;
I ponder long what Your hands
have wrought.
6 I stretch my hands to You;
My soul longs after You
As thirsts a dry and desert land.

7 Haste, LORD, to answer me!
O how my spirit fails!
Hide not the light of Your face
from me,
Lest I become like those
Who to the pit go down.
O let me not with them descend.

8 Let me Your mercy hear
When morning light appears;
I flee to You for my hiding place.
Teach me to know the way;
Show me how I should walk,
For I lift up my soul to You.

9 Deliver me, O LORD,
From all my enemies;
That You may hide me I flee
to You.
10 Teach me to do Your will;
My God of Spirit good,
O make me dwell in upright
lands.

11 For Your name's sake, O LORD,
Deal graciously with me;
Relieve my soul in Your
righteousness.
12 My foes slay in Your grace;
Destroy my enemies,
Because I am Your servant true.

TUNE: ST. ELIZABETH 669.668. (143C)
("Fairest Lord Jesus")

Psalm 144

1 Blessed be the LORD, my Rock,
Who trains my hands for war,
My fingers for the fight.
2 My Steadfast Love, my Fort,
My Stronghold, my Deliverer,
My Shield in Whom I refuge take,
He brings my people under me.

3 O LORD, what then is man
That You take note of him?
What is the son of man
That You consider him?
4 A breath, a nothingness is man.
As for the days of man, they all
Are like a shadow passing by.

5 O LORD, bow low Your heav'ns;
May You Yourself come down.
Yes, touch the mountaintops
And cause them thus to smoke.
6 Make lightning flash and
scatter them.
O may Your arrows be sent forth
To trouble and disquiet them!

7 Your hand send from on high
To rescue me and save
From waters great and deep,
From hands of alien folk,
8 Whose mouth speaks always
what is false,
And even the right hand of whom
Is a right hand of cunning lies.

(Continues)

121

9 O God, in praise to You,
   A new song I will sing.
   Upon a ten-stringed harp
   Your praises I will play.
10 For He salvation gives to kings;
   His servant David He will help
   And keep him from the
       wasting sword.

11 O rescue me and save,
   Grant me deliverance,
   From hands of alien folk,
   From power of foreigners,
   Whose mouth speaks always
       what is false,
   And even the right hand of whom
   Is a right hand of cunning lies.

12 So be our sons like plants
   Grown sturdy in their youth,
   And may our daughters be
   Like palace cornerstones;
13 All kinds of goods fill up
       our barns;
   Our flocks of sheep be multiplied
   By thousands and ten thousands
       more;

   Yes, may our cattle bear.
14 May there be no attacks,
   No going forth to war,
   No outcry in our streets.
15 O happy people who are thus!
   O happy people who can say
   They have the LORD to be
       their God!

   TUNE: PISGAH 66.66.888. (144C)

Psalm 145

Verses 1–10

1 I will Thee praise, my God,
       O King,
   And I will ever bless Thy name;
2 I will extol Thee every day
   And evermore Thy praise
       proclaim.
3 The LORD is great; He praise
       exceeds;
   His greatness fully search
       can none;
4 Race shall to race extol Thy deeds
   And tell Thy mighty acts
       each one.

5 Upon Thy glor-ious majesty
   And wondrous works my mind
       shall dwell;
6 Men shall recount Thy
       dreadful acts,
7 And of Thy greatness I will tell.
   They utter shall abundantly
   The mem'ry of Thy
       goodness great,
   And shall sing praises cheerfully
   While they Thy righteousness
       relate.

8 Jehovah very gracious is;
   In Him compassions also flow;
   In lovingkindness He is great,
   And unto anger He is slow.
9 O'er all His works His
       mercies are;
   The LORD is good to all that live.
10 Praise, LORD, to Thee Thy
       works afford;
   Thy saints to Thee shall
       praises give.

Verses 11–21

11 The glory of Thy kingdom show
   Shall they, and of Thy pow-er tell;
12 That so men's sons His deeds
       may know,
   His kingdom's glories that excel.

13 Thy kingdom has no end at all;
   It does through ages all remain.
14 The LORD upholdeth all that fall,
   The cast down raises up again.

15 The eyes of all upon Thee wait;
   Their food in season Thou
      dost give;
16 Thine opened hand doth satisfy
   The wants of all on earth that live.
17 The LORD is just in His ways all;
   In all His works His grace
      is shown;
18 The LORD is nigh to all that call,
   Who call in truth on Him alone.

19 He will the just desire fulfill
   Of such as do Him fear indeed;
   Their cry regard and hear He will,
   And save them in the time
      of need.
20 The LORD doth safely keep
      all those
   Who bear to Him a loving heart,
   But workers all of wickedness
   Destroy will He and clean subvert.

21 Then with my mouth and
      lips I will
   Jehovah's name with praise adore.
   And let all bless His holy name.
   Forever and for evermore.

TUNE: DUKE STREET LM (145A)
("Jesus Shall Reign")

Based on John Craig and
Scottish Psalter, 1564,
the *Book of Psalms*, 1871 and
The Psalter, 1912

Psalm 146

1 Hallelujah! Praise Jehovah!
   O my soul, Jehovah praise!
2 I will sing the glor-ious praises
   Of my God through all my days.
3 Put no confidence in princes,
   Nor for help on man depend;
4 He shall die, to dust returning,
   And his purposes shall end.

5 Happy is the man that chooses
   Jacob's God to be his aid;
   He is blessed whose hope
      of blessing
   On the LORD his God is stayed.
6 He has made the earth
      and heaven,
   Seas, and all that they contain;
   He will keep His truth forever,
7 Rights of those oppressed
      maintain.

   Food Jehovah gives the hungry,
   Sight Jehovah gives the blind,
   Freedom gives He to the pris'ner,
8 Cheer to those bowed down
      in mind.
   Well Jehovah loves the righteous
9 To the stranger is a stay,
   Helps the fatherless and widow,
   But subverts the sinner's way.

1 *Hallelujah, praise Jehovah,*
   O my soul, Jehovah praise;
2 *I will sing the glorious praises*
   Of my God through all my days.
10 Over all GOD reigns for ever,
   Through all ages He is King;
   Unto Him, thy God, O Zion,
   Joyful hallelujahs sing.

TUNE: RIPLEY 87.87.D
(new *Trinity Hymnal*, p. 57)

Based on the *Book of Psalms*, 1871, and
The Psalter, 1912; altered 1993

Psalm 147

Praise GOD! 'Tis good
  and pleasant,
And comely to adore;
Jehovah builds up Salem,
Her outcasts doth restore.
He heals the broken hearted,
And makes the wounded live;
4 The starry hosts He numbers,
And names to all doth give.

5 Our Lord is great and mighty;
His wisdom none can know;
6 The LORD doth raise the lowly
And sinners overthrow.
7 O thank and praise Jehovah!
Praise Him on harp with mirth,
8 The heav'n with clouds
    Who covers,
And sends His rain on earth.

9 He clothes with grass the
    mountains,
And gives the beasts their food;
He hears the crying ravens,
And feeds their tender brood.
10 In horse's strength delights not,
Nor speed of man loves He;
11 The LORD loves all who fear Him,
And to His mercy flee.

12 O Salem, praise Jehovah,
Thy God, O Zion, praise;
13 For He thy gates has
    strengthened,
And blessed thy sons with grace.
14 With peace He'll bless thy
    borders,
The finest wheat afford;
15 He sends forth His commandment,
And swiftly speeds His word.

16 Like wool the snow he giveth,
Spreads hail o'er all the land,
17 Hoarfrost like ashes scatters;
Who can His cold withstand?
18 Then forth His word he sendeth,
He makes His wind to blow;
The snow and ice are melted,
Again the waters flow.

19 The words that He has spoken
To Jacob He makes known;
His judgments and His statutes
To Is-ra-el has shown.
20 Not so to any nation
Did He His grace accord.
For they've not known His
    judgments.
O do ye praise the LORD.

TUNE: LANCASHIRE 76.76.D (31E)
  (new *Trinity Hymnal*, p. 580)
  ("Lead on O King Eternal")

Based on the *Book of Psalms,* 1871;
  vv. 19–20 altered 1994

Psalm 148

1 From heav'n O praise the LORD;
Ye heights, His glory raise.
2 All angels, praise accord;
Let all His host give praise.
3 Praise Him on high,
Sun, moon, and star,
Sun, moon, and star,
4 Ye heav'ns afar,
And cloudy sky.

5 Yea, let them glor-ious make
Jehovah's matchless name;
For when the word He spake
They into being came.
6 And from that place
Where fixed they be,
Where fixed they be,
By His decree
They cannot pass.

7 From earth O praise the LORD;
Ye deeps and all below;
8 Wild winds that do His word,
Ye clouds, fire, hail, and snow;
9 Ye mountains high,
Ye cedars tall.
Ye cedars tall,
10 Beasts great and small,
And birds that fly.

11 Let all the people praise,

And kings of ev'ry land;
Let all their voices raise
Who judge and give command.
12 By young and old,
By maid and youth,
By maid and youth,
13 His name in truth
Should be extolled.

Jehovah's name be praised
Above the earth and sky.
14 For He His saints has raised
And set their power on high.
Him praise accord,
O Isr'el's race,
O Isr'el's race,
Near to His grace.
Praise ye the LORD.

TUNE: ST. CATHERINES 66.66.44.44.
(148)

Elements from George Wither and
Scottish Psalter, 1650

Psalm 149

1 O praise ye the LORD! Prepare
your glad voice,
New songs with His saints
assembled to sing;
2 Before His Creator let Isr'el
rejoice,
And children of Zion be glad in
their King.

3 And let them His name extol in
the dance;
With timbrel and harp His praises
express;
4 Jehovah takes pleasure His saints
to advance,
And with His salvation the
humble to bless.

5 His saints shall sing loud with
glory and joy,
And rest undismayed; with songs
in the night
6 In praises to God they their lips
shall employ;

A sword in their right hand, two-
edg'd for the fight;
7 The heathen to judge, their pride
to consume,
8 To bind kings with chains, due
vengeance record,
9 To execute on them their long
decreed doom:
His saints have this honor. O
praise ye the LORD!

TUNE: LAUDATE DOMINUM 10.10.11.11.
(new *Trinity Hymnal*, p. 361)
("O Praise Ye the Lord")

The *Book of Psalms,* 1871

Psalm 150

1 Praise ye the LORD!
Praise unto God
Within His sanctuary raise.
Within His firmament of power
To Him on high O give ye praise.
2 O praise Him for His
mighty deeds,
For all His acts of providence.
O praise Him for His glory great
And for His matchless excellence.

3 O praise Him with the
trumpet sound.
Praise Him with rippling harp
and lyre.
4 Praise Him with timbrels in
the dance.
Praise Him with organ and
string choir.
5 Praise Him with cymbals
sounding high.
Praise Him with cymbals
clashing chord.
6 O praise the LORD, all things
that breathe!
O do ye praises give the LORD.

TUNE: CREATION LMD
(new *Trinity Hymnal*, p. 117)
Altered 1994

Tunes by Meter

The following list of tunes used in this book is organized by meter and includes the familiar words usually associated with the tune when there are such. When confronted with an unfamiliar tune and without access to music, another tune of the same meter may be substituted.

SM (6686)
Boylston *A Charge to Keep*		53
Festal Song *Rise Up O' Men of God*		108
Rialto		93
St. Michael		93
St. Thomas *I Love Thy Kingdom, Lord*		50
State Street		70
Terra Beata *This Is My Father's World*		11
Trentham *Breathe on Me Breath of God*		25

SMD
Diademata *All Hail the Power*	45
Leominster	16

CM (8686)
Abbeyville	125
Antioch *Joy to the World*	98
Arlington *This Is the Day*	26
Azmon *O for A Thousand Tongues*	133
Bangor	60
Beatitudo	69
Belmont *The Spirit Breathes Upon the Word*	12
Christmas	123
Crediton	59
Crimond	23
Culross	64
Desert	98
Downs	60
Dundee	121
Dunfermline	131
Effingham	77
Evan	17
Glasgow	127
Grafenberg	52
Horsley	22
Irish	95
Louise	52
Manoah	36
Martyrdom *Alas and Did*	130
Medfield	75
Meditation	119V
Miles Lane	66
Naomi	137
New Britain *Amazing Grace*	3
Olive's Brow	6
Richmond *City of God*	87

St. Agnes *Jesus the Very Thought*	42, 43
St. Anne *O God Our Help*	97
St. Flavian	62
St. Magnus *The Head that Once Was Crowned*	111
St. Martin's	117
St. Peter *In Christ There is No East*	119III
Salzburg	41
Winchester Old	125
Windsor	120

CMD
All Saints New *The Son of God Goes Forth to War*	110
Bethlehem	119IV
Ellacombe *Hosanna, Loud Hosanna*	78
Forest Green	37
Fountain *There Is a Fountain*	107
Halifax	140
Hetherton	21
Leveque	106
Maple Avenue	69
Materna *O Beautiful for Spacious Skies*	46
Myra	77
Noel	105
St. Asaph	118
St. Matthew	55
St. Michel's (Jerusalem)	58
Stockton *Only Trust Him*	119II
Vox Dilecti *I Heard the Voice of Jesus*	32
Weymouth	68
St. Asaph	118

LM (8888)
Canonbury *Lord Speak to Me*	141
Duke Street *Jesus Shall Reign*	145
Federal Street	132
Germany (Gardiner) *Where Cross the Crowded Ways*	57
Hamburg *When I Survey*	35
Hursley *Sun of My Soul*	138
Lasst uns erfreuen *All Creatures of Our God and King*	117
Llef	86
Maryton *O Master Let Me Walk*	139
Old 100th	100
Olive's Brow	6

Trinity Hymnal Tune References

The following numbers indicate the pages on which the listed tunes may be found in the *Trinity Hymnal*.

Mercy	333, 387, 673	St. Elizabeth	
Meribah		(similar Crusader's Hymn	170)
Merton		St. Flavian	589, 657
Miles Lane		St. George's Windsor	716
(similar	438)	St. John's	373
Missionary Hymn		St. Leonard	644
Monkland		St. Magnus	127, 298, 367
Morecambe	338, 378	St. Martin's	
Munich	140	St. Matthew	61, 470, 519
		St. Michael	78, 462
Naomi		St. Michel's	
Neander	324, 376, 453	St. Peter	647
Nettleton	457	St. Petersburg	88, 522, 635
New Britain/Amazing Grace	460	St. Thomas	353, 100
Noel	626	State Street	627
		Stockton/Minerva	675
Ode to Joy	122	Stuttgart	5
Old 100th	1, 100, 731	Sweet Hour	634
Old 110th			
Old 124th	614	Tallis Canon	401, 732
Olivette	528	Terra Beata	111
Olive's Brow	249	Toulon	168
Omni Die		Trentham	334, 516
		Trewen	463
Park Street	9, 19, 65	Truro	73, 198, 369
Penitence	532		
Penitentia		Vox Dilecti	304
Petersburg	88, 522		
Pilgrims		Wareham	
Pisgah	505	Webb	571
		Wesley LM	
Quebec/Hesperus	527, 610, 646, 712	Weymouth	
		Winchester New	58, 99, 394
Ravendale		Winchester Old	222
Regent Square	4, 218, 286, 342	Windsor	27
Redhead/Ajalon	335, 426, 486		
Rest CM		Yorkshire	209
Rest 8.6.8.8.6.			
Retreat	631		
Rialto			
Richmond	83		
Ripley	57, 80		
Rockingham Old	48, 422, 608		
Salvum Fac			
Salzburg			
Schmucke Dich			
(similar LMD	421)		
Spanish Hymn			
St. Agnes	332, 424, 645		
St. Anne	30, 713		
St. Asaph			
St. Bees	586		
St. Catherine	570		
St. Catherine's			
St. Christopher	251